THE
DAY
KHRUSHCHEV
FELL

Martin Page

THE
DAY
KHRUSHCHEV
FELL

Hawthorn Books, Inc., Publishers, New York

CONTENTS

Preface   9

1   October 15, 1964   11
2   Days by the Black Sea   21
3   Return to Moscow   33
4   Indictment and Defeat   50
5   Beginning of the End   66
6   Stalin's Crime   95
7   Behind the Fence   107
8   Outcry in the West   125
9   Revolt in the East   135
10 The Old Man   153
11 The New Men   169
12 The New Mood in Russia   190
13 Return to the Shadows   209

Index   217

CONTENTS

Preface

1.   11
2.
3.
4.   50
5.
6.
7.   107
8.   123
9.
10.
11.
12.   199
13.   205

Index   217

THE
DAY
KHRUSHCHEV
FELL

PREFACE

THIS ACCOUNT of recent events in Russia is unashamedly journalistic. Its purpose is not to contribute to the academic study of Soviet affairs, but to tell to a more general audience the story of how and why Khrushchev fell in October, 1964, and what happened as a result of his sudden disappearance from the political arena.

The sources which have been used in this reconstruction cannot be specified individually, but include Russians and foreigners living in Moscow, officials and others in the Communist countries of Eastern Europe, leaders of Western Communist parties who flew to Moscow to make their own investigations, and several foreign correspondents working for the British and American press who have been kind enough to contribute their observations. Less directly, we have drawn upon an intensive study of the Soviet press, on the reports of monitoring stations in the West, listening to broadcasts from the East, on accounts published in the Western press, particularly *The New York Times* and *Le Monde,* and on the deliberations of officials in Western foreign ministries.

"The foreign correspondent," another journalist has

written, "cannot aspire to the leisured certitude of the academic historian." Some professional Kremlinologists may disagree with some of the details of the story told. But no effort has been spared, within the difficult circumstances dictated by the Soviet Union's secrecy about its own affairs, to ensure the greatest possible degree of accuracy. It is the author's conviction that, whatever its defects, this account is the nearest it is possible at the present time to come to the truth about Khrushchev's fate.

1

OCTOBER 15, 1964

AT FIRST, nobody realized what a remarkable world scoop it was. Stories that Khrushchev had either died or been dismissed had come out of Moscow too often before, which had all proved later to be false; and when Victor Louis, a Russian who works there as a part-time correspondent for the *London Evening News*, telephoned the paper's head office at 1:40 P.M. London time, on October 15, 1964, he sounded calm and unexcited—in fact, to the duty foreign editor who took the call, rather boring. Louis often called at about that time, to offer safely nonpolitical features for the back pages of the next day's early editions, and on that day he seemed to be talking about the preparations for the welcome of the three cosmonauts who had just returned to earth after circling around it in one spacecraft.

Newspapers in London, as in the rest of the world, were already suffering from an amazing surfeit of news, and had little enthusiasm to receive any more. The British were at the polls, voting out the government that had ruled them for thirteen years. In America, Lyndon Johnson's self-confident election campaign was shaken severely by a sudden scandal: Walter Jenkins, the President's special assistant, had been arrested in the washroom of the Washington, D.C., YMCA and charged with "indecent gestures." The names of Nobel prizewinners were being announced in Stockholm; and in Tokyo, where the Olympic Games were in full swing, the British team had just won their second gold medal in two successive days.

The foreign editor listened half attentively to Louis (who refused to dictate a completed news story to a shorthand writer—for if he had done so and been wrong, it would have been a much greater offense in the eyes of Soviet officialdom than just mentioning the matter in "casual" conversation), and took some notes of what he said. They have been preserved in the *Evening News'* archives—as typed out by a secretary immediately afterward—and they read:

"Moscow is being decorated in preparation for welcoming the astronauts who come to the capital tomorrow. But missing from the usual portraits of government leaders is the well-known face of Mr. Khrushchev. Nobody knows anything for sure, but many Russians expect either today or at the latest tomorrow morning some explanation of a number of unusual events now taking place.

"Today's newspapers carry no mention of Mr. Khrushchev's name nor any quotation or his photograph. Moscow Radio is also not mentioning his name at all.

"Certainly the Soviet leader is alive, but these signs are quite usual ones here when the country's leaders are changing places.

"President Osvaldo Dorticos of Cuba arrived in Moscow on a state visit yesterday, but Mr. K. has not yet seen him and he was met and welcomed by the Soviet President Anastas Mikoyan."

With growing curiosity, the editor telephoned the British Embassy in Moscow (so giving diplomats there the first indication that Khrushchev had fallen—which they did not seem to take very seriously) and asked whether Khrushchev's portraits really had been removed. The political secretary who took the call had just driven back to the embassy after lunch at home, and assured him that the portraits were still in their usual positions. This later proved to be one of those occasions on which a journalist accidentally displays the true extent of his knowledge, by accurately reporting an event before it has happened.

Guessing that this might be so, the editor finally wrote a brief and cautious piece, by-lining it "From Our Special Correspondent, Moscow"; and at 4:00 P.M. it went on to the newsstands as the third most prominent story on the front page, under the headline "The Mystery of Mr. K."

Within thirty minutes, news agency flashes summarizing Louis' report were on the desk of virtually every important editor in the Western world. Unsure of how much trust they should place in it—the *Evening News* is not reputed for its foreign service—they reacted quickly but cautiously. Those with Moscow correspondents urgently telephoned or cabled them, demanding authoritative confirmation or denial. Soviet embassies in every major capital were besieged with calls of inquiry—but even if, incredibly, there were some Russian diplomat somewhere inclined to talk, he and his colleagues genuinely knew nothing.

In Moscow itself, the correspondents went through the routine farce of asking the Foreign Ministry's press department for information. In forty-five years of Communist rule no news has ever been obtained in this way.

But Westerners have stubbornly continued to ask their questions—if for no better reason than that they are expressly forbidden by the Foreign Ministry itself to put them to anybody else. The officials answered the first two or three callers by saying that they knew nothing —and then refused even to pick up their ringing phones.

In the streets, there were no signs of unusual activity, let alone tension. When Stalin had died eleven years before, thousands of troops patrolled the capital, and were stationed on the main squares. They had cordoned off the main thoroughfares, and in the panicking crowd several hundred people were crushed to death against the armored sides of riot trucks. Moscow itself was completely sealed off from the rest of the world for three days.

October 15 was one of the last autumnal days before winter set in, and huge crowds overflowed from the shops onto the pavements. But these people were far more concerned to find a pound of tomatoes, or a bunch of grapes, or some fresh fish for supper, than with the possibility of some political struggle which they could do nothing about. On Red Square, men and women in kapok jackets went on erecting the decorations for the cosmonauts' rally.

Then, two things happened. A woman came out of the *Izvestia* building in Pushkin Square and told the queue which forms there for the first edition every evening that there was to be no newspaper that night. And the correspondent of a foreign Communist newspaper quietly advised one of his bourgeois colleagues not to go far from a radio set during the evening. In the past, such incidents have been reliable indications that important news was about to break. Publication of *Izves-*

tia, the Government organ, was customarily delayed overnight on such occasions to stop it from scooping next morning's *Pravda,* which is the Party's main mouthpiece; and Communist correspondents were often extended the courtesy, denied to other Western journalists, of being alerted in the early evening to watch for special announcements near midnight, when the first editions of *Pravda* and the rescheduled *Izvestia* were coming from the presses.

But this scarcely amounted to confirmation of Louis' fantastic scoop. It was 7:00 P.M. in London and 9:00 P.M. in Moscow. Three hours had passed since the *Evening News* had first published it, and it was still the only news organ in the world to do so. On news desks in the West there was frustrated mystification. Their dealings with their Moscow correspondents have to be even more than normally cautious at times of political crisis, because all the lines of communication linking them are carefully monitored by the Soviet secret police. And these correspondents, without being able to explain why, were urging their editors not to print denials, but under no circumstances to publish confirmation.

Journalists in London, Paris, and New York who knew Victor Louis (and there were many) felt—although they were unable to act on the assumption—that he had to be right on account of his delicate position. Louis, now in his mid-thirties, is one of a tiny handful of Soviet citizens permitted to write for non-Communist publications in the West. Married to a Scottish girl who was once a nanny for a British Embassy family (they dismissed her when she refused to renounce her love for a Russian), he is the only one privileged to live in a "diplomatic house"—one of the blocks of apartments otherwise exclusively reserved for foreigners. Many of his Western friends believed that he had important contacts in the Communist party's Central Committee. He was not a man likely to take risks for the sake of a few dollars for, as well as all this, he started his adult life serving a ten-year sentence in a Siberian labor camp for a political offense.

But if his story was at least basically true, what had in fact happened? Was Khrushchev dead or perhaps incurably ill? Or had he stepped down from his position as First Secretary of the Communist party or as Prime Minister, as a first move toward honorable and long-rumored retirement? Or had he been removed by some sinister—possibly Stalinist, pro-Chinese—*coup d'état?* Above all, would there be a proper explanation before the end of the night? Newspapers called in their Soviet experts, dusted their obituaries, and, in the informational vacuum, started to prepare articles suitable for any of these contingencies, to be ready for publication the moment any sort of official announcement was made.

Apart from this, they could do little but try to find sublimation in the harassment of their Moscow correspondents—which was, of course, the last thing these people needed. Unlike their colleagues at home, they dared not speculate in writing, for fear that it would result—in the event of their being wrong—either in their immediate expulsion from the Soviet Union or in the total closure of their organization's bureau—most probably in both. The majority of them worked under the order not to allow this to happen at almost any cost— even that of suppressing news; and their memories of a similar evening, not many months before, were frighteningly fresh. Through a series of strange and grave mistakes, the usually excellent West German news agency DPA had sent out a flash to its subscribers, saying that TASS had announced Khrushchev's death. Moscow correspondents received panic-stricken calls from their editors, and checked their own TASS teleprinters. These had received nothing of the sort, but they had gone dead two hours previously, halfway through a report of a speech Khrushchev was making at a dinner in the Kremlin, in honor of the visiting Polish leader, Wladislaw Gomulka. The transmission had ended ominously with the word "more"—followed by silence.

It was hours before a firm denial could be obtained from any responsible Soviet official. Several were willing to say that he was in good health and humor at the dinner, but they all failed to state categorically that he was still alive. Only in the early hours of the morning did the director-general of TASS, Dmitri Goryunov, finally receive instructions from above and telephone Western news agencies asking them to distribute a statement saying the report was "absolute rubbish." (The TASS wire itself failed to issue any denial, for fear of giving further currency to the original rumor.) Going to a Polish Embassy reception the next evening, Khrushchev deliberately made great play of his first public appearance since the report: he got out of his limousine on the side away from the pavement and spent perhaps half a minute smiling and waving his hat at the crowd. Inside the reception itself, the director of the Foreign Ministry's press department, Leonid Zamyatin, angrily went up to Western reporters to accuse their German colleague of "deliberate provocation." Next morning, ignoring the repeated groveling and frightened apologies

which had been pouring out of the agency's headquarters in Hamburg, cordoned off by the police as an
investigation went on inside, Zamyatin gave its Moscow
correspondent twenty-four hours to close the bureau
and leave the country. This was viciously short notice:
the usual term was two weeks; and it was in spite of the
fact that it could be easily established—through record-
ings of international telephone calls—that he knew nothing of the message when it was sent out, and that when
he was told, he did his utmost to have it immediately
denied.

Sam Jaffe of the American Broadcasting Company
was in a better position than most of his rivals to investigate the rumors. In contrast with many other American
correspondents, who had been effectively discouraged
from making close Soviet contacts because of the ex-
traordinary difficulties and suspicions involved on both
sides, Jaffe had created good relationships with a number of Russians—including a few senior officials. The
success of his policy was proved when, at 5:04 P.M., he
became the first Westerner to report, without reservation, that Khrushchev had fallen, together with his
closest personal advisers. Henry Shapiro, the Moscow
bureau chief of United Press International and the
doyen (by virtue of the thirty-two years he has served
in Moscow) of the Western press corps, followed his
example at 7:27 P.M.

Other correspondents sought external signs of upheaval. They had already noticed an unusual gathering
of the black *Chaika* (Seagull) limousines with which
senior Soviet ministers and functionaries are provided,
parked outside the grim, gray party Central Committee
building on Staraya Square. They checked back num-

bers of *Pravda* and other newspapers and found that the formal messages of greeting to the cosmonauts earlier that week lacked the customary signatures of N. S. Khrushchev and were attributed impersonally to the Central Committee; and also that Khrushchev had not spoken on the phone to the cosmonauts on their return, as he had invariably done with their predecessors.

Final indirect confirmation came a few minutes after 10:00 P.M. in Moscow. Workmen appeared in front of the skyscraper Moskva Hotel, scaled its front wall—facing the Kremlin—and began to dismantle the huge portrait of Khrushchev that had for some months darkened the windows of the bedrooms facing that way. After that, reports that Khrushchev was definitely out rushed through the telephone, cable and teleprinter wires to the outside world.

But hesitation came jolting back. Andrei Smirnov, the Soviet Ambassador in Bonn, attending a reception, said the reports were "in the realm of speculation." A TASS editor telephoning from Paris said, "I know nothing about any such rumors."

Teleprinters receiving the TASS international service finally jumped to life a few minutes after it was midnight in Moscow—and two minutes after the first result of the British general election was declared—to state in clumsy but clear English:

"Moscow, October 16—Nikita Khrushchev has been released of the duties as the First Secretary of the CPSU Central Committee and chairman of the Council of Ministers of the U.S.S.R. Leonid Brezhnev has been elected First Secretary of the CPSU Central Committee. Alexei Kosygin has been appointed chairman of the Council of Ministers.

"It has been announced today that a plenary meeting of the CPSU Central Committee held on Wednesday, October 14, considered Khrushchev's request to be relieved of his duties 'in view of his advanced age and deterioration of his health.'

"An official announcement about the plenary meeting of the CPSU Central Committee which was made public reads: 'A plenary meeting of the Central Committee of the CPSU was held on October 14. The meeting granted N. S. Khrushchev's request to be relieved of his duties as the First Secretary of the CPSU Central Committee, member of the Presidium of the CPSU Central Committee, and chairman of the Council of Ministers of the U.S.S.R. in view of his advanced age and deterioration of his health.

"'The plenum of the CPSU Central Committee elected L. I. Brezhnev First Secretary of the CPSU Central Committee.'"

In response to the rumors, share prices on the New York Stock Exchange had already fallen by 11.23 points during the early afternoon. Now, those on the San Francisco Stock Exchange—the biggest Western one still open, on account of the time difference—tumbled still further. It was an ironic initial response to the fall of the sworn enemy of capitalism.

2

DAYS BY THE
BLACK SEA

THE PEOPLE who stormed the battlements of Russian secrecy in October and November, 1964, were neither diplomats nor journalists, but Communist leaders from the West who refused to be satisfied with the bare announcement they had been given, and flew to Moscow to demand a full explanation.

In Moscow, they were met one after another by members of the Presidium and were told that it would be "inadvisable" at the present time to disclose what had taken place. Several disagreed, including the delegation of British Communists who went there to inquire into the matter, and decided to pass on what they had been told to a wider audience in their own countries. To a large extent, the following reconstruction has been based on their various findings and reports, although information from the widest possible range of other sources has been incorporated as well. These range from newspaper clippings to a semisecret account produced by a Western Foreign Ministry for the use of its officials, from the observations of correspondents to stories circulating in Warsaw, Budapest and other East European capitals. Much of it will not be new to experts, but it is perhaps the first time that ordinary readers in the West have been given such a report. The reservations the reader should make in considering its reliability should be obvious; there can be little doubt that, in spite of all the efforts that have been made to ensure accuracy, some of the evidence has been distorted on its way from Moscow, and some of the deductions which have been made from it will be inevitably wrong as a result. But there is equally little doubt that it is an essentially faithful account of what happened during the fifteen crucial days.

Nikita Sergeyevich Khrushchev left Moscow in his position as First Secretary of the Soviet Communist party and Chairman of the Council of Ministers of the U.S.S.R. for the last time on September 30. He traveled south across Russia for two nights and one day in his private train (he disliked flying increasingly), accompanied only by his personal staff, to the Black Sea resort of Gagra. From there, he went the last eighteen miles by car to his favorite retreat, his villa at Cape Pitsunda, nearby. Before he departed from the capital, he had himself created the circumstances in which his opponents, who had been discussing his overthrow for months, could at last succeed.

He was tired and, almost certainly, still irritated by the stubborn resistance with which his colleagues were blocking the execution of his latest schemes for economic reform. But he clearly felt no fear for his future—otherwise he would never have left his office in the Kremlin in the first place. This seemed to him to be a routine journey in the pattern which had become increasingly familiar to him as he had grown older and had begun to lack the stamina to direct the nation's affairs from Moscow without frequent breaks.

In the last years of his reign, his life had taken on a
bimonthly rhythm similar to that which more normal
people experience every twenty-four hours: arriving in
his office refreshed from his latest holiday, he would
plunge into his work for five or six uninterrupted, grueling weeks (often putting in as many as eighteen hours
in a single day) before he brought himself once again
near the point of total exhaustion. Then, he would take
himself away to recover, and build up the energy he
would need to survive the next stint in Moscow. Sometimes—particularly in the winter—he went to Zavidovo,
a hunting lodge normally reserved for foreign diplomats
on the banks of the Volga about a four-hour drive from
Moscow, to shoot elk and wild boar. Occasionally, he
went to Kiev, to the house overlooking the Dnieper
River, from which he had ruled the Ukraine on Stalin's
behalf before and during the war. But most often—as on
this last trip—he went to Cape Pitsunda, where the
weather was warmer, his villa more luxurious, and
where facilities were permanently installed—including
an extension to the emergency hot line linking the
Kremlin with the White House—for doing any urgent
business of state that could not be put off until the
return to Moscow.

This was probably the most magnificent private residence still in use in the whole of the Soviet Union. Few
Russians even knew of its existence—let alone dreamed
of its opulence—but Khrushchev loved to invite foreign
and particularly Western visitors down there to show it
off.

Surrounded on three sides by a state farm, and half
concealed from prying eyes by a wood of rare prehis-
toric pine trees, it was finally sealed off from the outside

world by an ugly concrete wall, ten feet high. The house itself was a severe, Soviet contemporary sandstone cube with a garden and a mock-Japanese teahouse on its roof, two stories above the ground. A glass-walled terrace along its front overlooked the sheltered private bay where, with a large black rubber ring fixed around his middle (for he was not a confident swimmer), Khrushchev sometimes bathed. Most of the time, he preferred to use the seventy-five-foot heated swimming pool connected by a corridor with the house. In good weather —as Khrushchev demonstrated to visitors on every possible occasion—it could be opened to the fresh air at the touch of a button, at which the steel and glass walls would slide away. To the side of the house, there was a covered recreation area, with picture windows running the length of its walls, and including a gymnasium carpeted with valuable oriental rugs, where Khrushchev used to exercise himself privately with dumbbells and medicine balls, and play badminton with his guests. Telephones were everywhere—in boxes fixed to the trees along the paths where he used to walk; by the swimming pool; in the gym; and there was even a white one, directly connected with the secret Government exchange in the Kremlin, in the bathing hut where he used to change on the beach.

Except for the absence of Nina Petrovna, his wife (who usually accompanied him)—she was taking the waters at a spa in Czechoslovakia—the first twelve days of Khrushchev's stay were fairly routine. There were few visitors with whom he had to talk business, the international situation was reasonably calm, and his most pressing task was to prepare a speech to give to a special plenum of the Central Committee on agricultural matters.

In Moscow, all was as outwardly calm as Western newspapermen had come to expect during the "old man's" absences. Many of Khrushchev's colleagues—including Leonid Brezhnev, his heir apparent in the party, and Nikolai Podgorny, his second lieutenant in party affairs—were out of town themselves, on their last excursions before the winter set in. But among those politicians who remained in the Kremlin, the final, but still inconclusive, discussions about a plot to overthrow him had begun.

Anastas Mikoyan, the longest-surviving politician in the Communist world, whom Khrushchev had recently placed in honorable semiretirement as Soviet President, flew the fifteen hundred miles to the Black Sea coast on October 3 (when Khrushchev had been there little more than twenty-four hours) to warn him that his colleagues were in earnest over their objections to his policies, and to plead for compromise. A delegation of French Communists, who went to Moscow soon afterwards to demand explanations for Khrushchev's overthrow, were told that the purpose of Mikoyan's mission was to "tell Comrade Khrushchev that the present position of the Presidium [the eleven-member body which effectively rules the Soviet Communist party and, through it, the state] should be reconsidered."

This cautious phrase concealed the two explosive topics which dominated their discussion. Khrushchev had—fatally, as it turned out—rejected the strongly held opinions of the majority of his colleagues and loudly insisted that his view be accepted. He had then gone on holiday assuming that, while they would complain among themselves about his dictatorial behavior for a while, they would eventually fall back into line rather than create an open division—particularly at a time when Soviet dominance of the world Communist movement was being challenged so gravely in Asia.

The first dispute was over his plan for yet another reorganization of the country's chaotic agriculture. Khrushchev's fascination with farming was a joke that had by now become bitter to the whole nation; and, after the disastrous harvest of the previous autumn, his colleagues were in no mood to humor him further. With the exception of the Virgin Lands (Khrushchev's personal project to create a harvest out of waste land and which resulted in colossal failure the previous autumn), grain yields in most areas were much higher in 1964 than they had been in 1963, but still considerably below the minimum Russia needed to be self-supporting in its food production. Twelve months had passed since the Virgin Lands catastrophe and there was still no flour in the shops, and the supply of white bread was erratic in the capital and worse elsewhere.

Khrushchev, as undeterred by the growing exasperation as he was by the failure of all his previous policies, intended to put forward his new scheme of reform to a special plenum of the Communist party's Central Committee on his return to Moscow.

It was based, in common with its predecessors, on a reorganization of agricultural management. Earlier, he had placed the responsibility in the hands of the collective farmers themselves; then, disillusioned by the new inefficiencies and shortages this move created, he transferred it to the party officials who were themselves reorganized into agricultural and industrial units to take on the task. But they proved to be too bureaucratic to achieve anything but the construction of new obstacles to the development of whatever efficient farming units there were. So he had turned once more to the farmers themselves.

All this having failed, he decided that a completely new administrative structure was needed, and he now proposed that the Soviet Union be divided into seventeen huge, semiautonomous agricultural regions with the equivalent of a provincial governor in charge of each. They were to be co-ordinated by an agricultural "king" who was to be installed in the Kremlin.

To Leonid Brezhnev, Alexei Kosygin and the rest, this was futile, because too many such managerial reforms had been instituted in the past to no effect, and was irrelevant, because it avoided the basic issue. Brezhnev, as the man who had been appointed by Khrushchev to get the Virgin Lands scheme under way and who had been in charge of it during its initial successes, and Kosygin, as an economist disturbed by the repeated pattern of new crises emerging after every change, felt that they had a clear understanding of the heart of the agricultural problem; but Khrushchev refused to accept their views. Nobody disputed that his judgment was correct, so far as it stressed the gross mismanagement, the lack of mechanization and the poor selection of seed varieties. But the central problem was otherwise: the majority of peasants working on state and collective farms saw no reason to exert themselves on the nationally or communally owned land, when they could earn a greater income by working on their small private plots, and selling their produce independently. The only answer to this attitude, Brezhnev and Kosygin argued, was to make it more profitable to work communally on the land, rather than individually. Then the problem would solve itself.

Such reasoning was distasteful to Khrushchev, partly, perhaps, because he found it ideologically suspect (he used to react in a violently socialistic way when Western capitalists suggested that private plots were flourishing while collective and state farms stagnated) and partly because—like so many Russians who had moved from the country into industrial towns in the past fifty years —he had developed a highly sentimentalized view of the peasant. Indeed, he considered himself essentially to be one: warm and hospitable, yet blunt and straightforward, honest and reliable, and endowed with a natural wisdom which comes from communion with the soil. He felt himself far more at home on visits to the country than he did in the Kremlin, where he found life circumscribed by an irksome alien protocol. And so any attack on the peasantry—which he considered this to be—he took as an attack upon himself.

He was not only determined that his plan should go through with or without the approval of the Presidium; he was also insistent that it should be run not by Government or party officials but by a personal protégé, who would presumably be responsible solely to him. He had nominated his extremely unpopular son-in-law, Alexei Adzhubei, for the task.

Adzhubei lacked any apparent qualification for this job. His only official position (through which he had also become a member of the Central Committee) was editor of the Government newspaper *Izvestia;* and as such, he had earned himself considerable credit both inside and outside the Soviet Union for the vitality he had brought to the otherwise overwhelmingly moribund field of Russian journalism. But his unofficial position, so obviously founded on the nepotism he had been able to exploit since he married Khrushchev's daughter Rada (then at Moscow University), was resented. He was the most intimate and influential of Khrushchev's advisers, and through him Khrushchev had increasingly attempted to bypass official channels. One Russian official privately compared him to an evil dwarf whispering into the emperor's ear; and members of his own staff on *Izvestia* used to joke openly that when Khrushchev went Adzhubei would be "promoted" to the control of the second most important newspaper in Vladivostok. (In fact, he was made literary editor of a glossy magazine.)

Personally popular in the West, because of the contrast his easygoing behavior made with the cold awkwardness of many of his compatriots abroad, his unashamed passion for high living caused great offense at home. On one recorded occasion, in the course of a campaign against teen-age drunkenness, in which his newspaper had played an active part, he demanded and after a lengthy dispute with the manager was finally served a bottle of brandy in a youth café where hard liquor had been banned. When abstract artists were suffering mild persecution—in that they were publicly rebuked and stopped from exhibiting or selling their works—through his father-in-law's decree, Adzhubei openly boasted of his own private collection of such paintings.

Probably the greatest embarrassment he caused the authorities was when he persuaded the Moscow City Soviet (Council) to build a small block of apartments whose opulence would rival that of Mayfair or Park

Avenue. He was to live in one, and the remaining ones were to be reserved for other members of Khrushchev's entourage. Building work began in the autumn of 1962, on a site opposite the East German Embassy. Then, the construction workers saw the plans: each apartment was to have seven large rooms, occupying a whole floor to itself, and three terraces (so that the sun, when it shone, could be enjoyed at almost any time of the day). These workers themselves, like millions of their fellow Muscovites, were living in a cramped squalor unimaginable to most Western visitors, who see only the outside of the huge new blocks of apartment buildings shooting up all over Moscow. Theoretically, these contained two- or three-room apartments; in fact, this meant that their families—frequently comprising three generations from grandparents to grandchildren—lived in one small room and shared a kitchen and bathroom with two other, similarly accommodated, families. They went on strike—in spite of the fact that such an act is punishable with banishment to Siberia or another part of the Far East. Fortunately for them, those responsible for rebuking them secretly understood the justice of their case, and their punishment was said to have been a token one. The block of apartments was completed by the next spring and stands almost empty today as a monument to Adzhubei's ostentation.

To the Soviet hierarchy, any suggestion that Adzhubei's power should be other than diminished was intolerable. According to persistent Moscow gossip, Khrushchev's colleagues had defeated a proposal to give official recognition to his role as Khrushchev's personal envoy to the West by kicking Andrei Gromyko upstairs to a deputy-premiership and appointing Adzhubei For-

eign Minister in his place. Khrushchev had apparently
given way. This time, whether blinded by personal affection or simply stubborn, he decided that he would
not; and not even Anastas Mikoyan, the Armenian grand
master of political compromise, sitting with him on the
terrace overlooking the Black Sea, could dissuade him.

At this key meeting at Cape Pitsunda on October 3,
the two men turned to the most crucial issue, which is
still and is likely to be for many years to come, central
to Soviet politics—the lagging economy. Khrushchev's
new economic plan was couched in abstruse terminol-
ogy, but its basis was radically simple: he wanted to
accelerate the development of light industry by pouring
into it massive amounts of public capital that previously
had been allocated to the development of the munitions
and heavy industries. He considered these last two to be
adequately developed to fulfill the nation's essential requirements in the immediate future, and felt that the
time had come to balance them with rapid expansion
in other fields. Because ever-increasing capital investment in heavy industry had become all but an article
of faith to Russian politicians, other sections of the
economy had been consistently deprived of the money
they needed for the past forty-five years. Khrushchev's
plan had the incidental advantage of providing a boost
for his diminishing popularity, by producing an unprecedented supply of consumer goods.

In the third week of September, just before Khrushchev left Moscow, the Presidium had held a meeting
with the Council of Ministers and Gosplan, the state
planning board which, under Alexei Kosygin's direction,
was charged with the over-all responsibility for the national economy. The purpose of the meeting was to

agree upon the final directives for the new five-year plan, due to start in 1966.

Kosygin, speaking for the planning board, presented the final draft of its proposal, which directly contradicted Khrushchev's. Italian Communists were told later that he had rejected them completely in a long and violent speech. Khrushchev's opposition was determined that the expansion of basic industries—such as mining and iron and steel production—should not be dependent on their future ability to finance themselves out of their profits. They also saw little point in creating an artificial boom in light industry when the factories which already existed in this field were running with such outrageous inefficiency that warehouses all over urban Russia were crammed with unsalable but brand-new junk that had cost tens of millions of dollars to produce, and that had once borne the title of consumer goods but had never even reached the shops. Again, they felt, Khrushchev was refusing to face the real and extremely disturbing issues affecting the survival of the Soviet state, while occupying himself with trifles.

Khrushchev, it is said, was not willing to even discuss the possibility of a compromise and seemed to feel that the others were merely demonstrating their weakness by proposing one. Nevertheless, the meeting ended with the passing of a formal motion instructing the planning board to devise a new, middle-of-the-road plan that could satisfy the convictions and the honor of both sides. Such a directive was clearly impossible to carry out, however much Kosygin wanted to succeed. Khrushchev had created a situation in which one side had to win, and the other to lose.

3

RETURN TO MOSCOW

AT HALF PAST ten on the morning of Monday, October 12, with a great blast of white-hot flame, the world's first multipassenger spaceship blasted itself off its launching pad at the Baikonur spacedrome in Central Asia. Inside the cramped cabin of the huge, seven-ton craft—called *Voskhod I* (Sunrise I)—were the latest heroes of the Soviet space program: pilot Vladimir Komarov, physicist Constantin Feoktistov and physician Boris Yegorov. As *Voskhod's* powerful gas rockets lifted it outside the pull of gravity and into orbit, a record-breaking 254 miles above the surface of the earth, Komarov reported over the radio that "all was fine"; and the three men began to prepare to spend a week together in space.

For the Soviet scientists watching and listening in their remote headquarters below, it was a triumphant proof of their claim to be two years ahead of their American rivals at Cape Kennedy. This was also the very kind of success that particularly exhilarated Mr. Khrushchev—and the sort of justification he had prayed for when he had first initiated the fantastic campaign to win national prestige through cosmic technology.

He had claimed in a recent speech that Westerners had looked on Russia before its successes in space as little more than "a nation of peasants who drink cabbage soup out of leaking straw boots." The first cosmonaut, Yuri Gagarin, and his successors had dramatically shaken them out of their antisocialist fixations, he claimed. "You can't drink soup out of your straw boots up there—it's outside the pull of gravity!" Khrushchev mimicked the incredulous capitalists of his imagination as crying.

On this particular day, he had himself connected with the spaceship by radio-telephone at 1:00 P.M.—the first possible moment after the success of the flight had been announced to the world by TASS and Radio Moscow. He was still at Cape Pitsunda, and in jubilant spirits, promising the three men a "welcome greater than the force of gravity" when they returned to earth the next weekend.

This conversation with the cosmonauts was televised in his study overlooking the sea. It was his last public appearance as Soviet leader and these were his last recorded words to the people he had ruled for almost ten years. They were strangely, if unknowingly, prophetic: "Here's Comrade Mikoyan. He's grabbing the phone out of my hands. I don't think I can stop him," he said. And his famous face, laughing hugely at his own joke, disappeared forever from the screen.

If Western correspondents watching the program in Moscow were surprised to see Anastas Mikoyan in Cape Pitsunda when his official program, as the newly elected President of the Soviet Union, was so heavy and his health so poor (he was suffering from a chronic liver complaint), they thought little more of it at the time.

In fact, this mission was his decisive one: the second, fruitless and final, attempt to persuade Khrushchev that it was foolhardy to ignore a moment longer the resistance of his colleagues to his economic and agricultural reform plans, and that he should return to Moscow and attempt to reach a compromise with them before it was too late.

According to the account given later by people who were directly involved in Khrushchev's overthrow, Mikoyan warned him that the opposition was becoming more and more entrenched in the capital for every day he delayed his return. It was no longer simply a question of the development of heavy or light industry being favored in the future, or whether Adzhubei was to be put in charge of agricultural reorganization. Old issues were being revived now—such as his frustrated attempt to have members of the "antiparty group," including Molotov and Bulganin, publicly tried for treason instead of being merely dismissed—and a new and more general complaint was gathering force: his own increasingly dogmatic behavior and his drift toward absolute dictatorship. Mikoyan also mentioned the Virgin Lands scheme and said that some members of the Presidium were determined to scrap it.

Khrushchev had heard such stories many times before. He saw no reason to believe on this occasion that the situation was any more threatening now than it had been during several more dramatic crises in the past. Indeed, to such a master politician viewing his opposition from the Black Sea coast, it seemed to be a comparatively easy corner out of which he could fight his way in his own time.

Mikoyan flew back alone, his loyalty to his old friend

exhausted and discharged. He reached Moscow in the late afternoon of the twelfth and, Western intelligence accounts state, a meeting of the Presidium was called almost immediately to hear his report. Mikoyan said that his attempt to mediate between them and Khrushchev had failed and that, from now on, he could be counted as one of the anti-Khrushchev majority. It is not known how long into the night the meeting continued, but it was certainly during the course of it that Khrushchev's colleagues resolved, in principle, to overthrow him as soon as possible. With immediate effect, they issued two orders to Central Committee officials waiting outside: first, Khrushchev's name was to be deleted from all messages coming in, congratulating the Soviet Union on its latest success in space, before they were passed on to the press for publication. (The revealing discrepancy this produced, between newspapers in Hungary, for example, printing the text of a message from Janos Kadar congratulating "Comrade N. S. Khrushchev, First Secretary of the Communist Party of the Soviet Union," and newspapers in Russia readdressing the remarks, in their reports, to "The Central Committee of the Communist Party of the Soviet Union," was not noticed by Western observers until after the official announcement it foreshadowed.) Second, the spacecraft itself was to return to earth as soon as it was light. For the Presidium members felt that it would be embarrassing to have it blazing a trail of publicity over the Soviet Union, while the Government below was overthrown.

At this point, an incongruous but extremely useful figure entered the story. M. Gaston Palewsky, the French minister for atomic energy, was on an official visit to the Soviet Union, to discuss exchanges of information on the peaceful uses of nuclear power. He had been invited to lunch with Khrushchev at Cape Pitsunda on Wednesday the thirteenth, and spent the night of October 12 in a hotel at the nearby resort of Sochi.

He was unexpectedly telephoned at seven-thirty in the morning, to be told that Khrushchev would be unable to receive him for lunch because the cosmonauts were about to land, and he would have to rush back to Moscow to greet them. The Chairman presented his apologies, his secretary told Palewsky, and invited him to call for a talk instead at half-past nine.

In fact, the cosmonauts had landed with such haste that the spacecraft had missed the target area by several hundred miles; and as Palewsky was being driven along the coast road to Cape Pitsunda, they were awaiting rescue in the middle of a remote Central Asian plain. In spite of TASS's (its initials in Russian stand for the Telegraph Agency of the Soviet Union) bland claim later that morning, when it belatedly announced the news of the cosmonauts' return after only twenty-four hours in orbit, that this had been "fully in accordance with the plan," it clearly had not been. That day's *Pravda*, containing the altered messages of congratulation, was still being read at breakfast tables all over the country, and it was still speaking of a week's stay in space. Moscow Television, after showing a live transmission from the spacecraft's cabin the evening before, had promised that its engineers would attempt another linkup with "cosmovision" the following afternoon. Space scientists in the West found the return inexplicable, and tentatively suggested that one of the cosmonauts might have fallen ill, or that the cabin—whose temperature had been reported two degrees centigrade above normal the previous day—might have become dangerously overheated.

When a second hint of the significance of this event came in the afternoon, it was too obscure for anybody to understand by itself. Russian journalists accredited to the space program and allowed access (strictly forbidden to their foreign colleagues) to the spacedrome at Baikonur reported in the evening newspapers a strange radio conversation between its director, the anonymous "chief engineer," and pilot Komarov, while the *Voskhod* was still in orbit. When the former ordered Komarov to bring his spacecraft back to earth immediately, he remonstrated and pointed out that he and his crew had not yet had time to carry out a large number of the observations they had been instructed to make. The chief engineer replied that he understood their feelings and appreciated their devotion to their task. He paused for a moment, and then added enigmatically: "There are more things in heaven and earth than are dreamt of in your philosophy. Come down."

When Palewsky arrived at the villa, he was taken straight into Khrushchev's study. He noted that his host was slightly nervous and restless, although not excessively so. The first half hour of conversation between the two men passed amiably enough (President de Gaulle was beginning to seek an *entente* with Russia then) but a few minutes after 10:00 A.M., the meeting came to an abrupt and dramatic end. The door opened, and an official rushed into the room, going straight up to Khrushchev. He spoke to him in an urgent undertone for a few moments and then, without more ado, he ushered Palewsky straight out of the room and into a car outside, scarcely pausing to apologize.

Khrushchev himself was driven straight to the nearest airport, at Adler, to find that his private plane had disappeared with its crew. Unknown to him, another plane with a strange crew had been sent from Moscow to collect him. This was probably the first unmistakable sign to Khrushchev that he was no longer in control; but he flew back to the capital determined to fight nevertheless.

In Moscow, the Presidium had been meeting for most of the morning of the thirteenth. Leonid Brezhnev, Khrushchev's long-serving lieutenant, who had been deputed by him to supervise party affairs during his absence, was in the chair. Seven of the other ten members were seated at the table before him: Alexei Kosygin, the nation's economic overlord; Anastas Mikoyan; Mikhail Suslov, the thin, ascetic director of ideological affairs, whose main preoccupation was the dispute with the Chinese; Nikolai Podgorny, the secretary for light industry and trade; Gennadi Voronov, who ran the party machine within the Russian Federation; the old and by now largely inactive trade union leader Nikolai Shvernik; Andrei Kirilenko, a professional party organizer; and Dmitri Potansky, at forty-seven by far the youngest man in the group. Of the three absentees, one was known to be a sympathizer with Khrushchev's opposition: Frol Koslov, who was able to play no active part in the coup because he had been paralyzed a year before by a stroke affecting the whole of the left side of his body.

Mikhail Suslov is believed to have spoken first. He was one of Khrushchev's most consistent and longest-standing opponents, who had several times gone out of his way to demonstrate his disdain for the First Secretary in public, and even in the presence of foreigners. Descended from a family of Old Believers—an extremist religious sect which broke away from the Russian Orthodox Church in the seventeenth century rather than accept the modernization of the liturgy ordered by the Patriarch—he had inherited all their puritanical fervor, but expressed it in a Marxist-Leninist context. He disapproved of Khrushchev's peasant familiarity and ebullience: once, for example, he ordered the orchestra at a Kremlin ball, against Khrushchev's own wishes, to moderate its tone and play in a "more seemly fashion." On another occasion, when a visiting photographer innocently asked for his help in obtaining permission to photograph a meeting of the Presidium, he replied: "No. I shall not pass on your request to Comrade Khrushchev because I very much doubt that he would refuse."

Suslov had achieved his position under Stalin and owed nothing to Khrushchev, throughout whose rule he had advocated greater orthodoxy in executing the theories of Marxism-Leninism and stricter organization of the nation's affairs. His detailed indictment of Khrushchev now ranged from the "undemocratic" methods he had used to gain power in the first place, through his mismanagement of industry and agriculture and his capricious conduct of foreign affairs, to his histrionic mishandling of the crisis in relations with Peking (his near-obscene attack on Mao Tse-tung, as a man "with a worm wriggling and writhing in his arse-hole," had caused almost as universal offense in Russia as it had in China), to his creation of a cult of personality around himself, after he had condemned Stalin for doing the same.

But all this was little more than a formality and, perhaps, a rehearsal of his more public condemnation of the party's First Secretary before the Central Committee which was to take place forty-eight hours later. Any traces of indecision that might have been in the minds of the eight men had evaporated overnight. Discussion was no longer on the question of whether they should overthrow Khrushchev but on how it was to be done. Precise and careful planning was essential before they took any further action: Khrushchev, who justifiably prided himself on his skill as a political tactician, had successfully defeated similar attempts to overthrow him before, usually by bypassing the Presidium and putting his case directly to the three hundred and thirty members of the Communist party's Central Committee. On each occasion, he had made an appeal for their support through popular acclaim and had been given a rousing response. He had most recently employed this device in the dispute over relations with China. At a special meeting of the Central Committee in February, 1964, Suslov had presented a long, secret report to the delegates, describing the current state of relations between the two parties, and outlining in strong terms the Russian case against the Chinese. Khrushchev had moved that the report should be published. Other members of the Presidium opposed him, arguing that the only result of such a move would be to give the Chinese an opportunity to claim that the Russians were guilty of gratuitous provocation, at a time when they themselves were attempting to practice self-restraint. Khrushchev continued to insist on publication and finally threatened to resign if he did not get his way. A vote was taken, and he was overwhelmingly defeated. But instead of resigning (a move which his colleagues, of course, would have welcomed), he stood up again, and made another speech, cataloguing his virtues, expressing his devotion to the Soviet people and the "party of Lenin" and pleading for a mandate to continue. Once again, the formula had worked.

Another recent attempt to overthrow him—early in 1963—also provided them with an object lesson in failure. The fault then had been the lack of organization and of an outwardly united front against Khrushchev within the Presidium—although most of its members seemed to be already in private agreement that the time had come for him to go. The main complaint they had then was against Khrushchev's apparent interpretation of the meaning of "collective leadership," the oligarchical form of government which had theoretically replaced Stalin's tyranny. It seemed to them that he took this to mean that he made all the decisions personally, and the Presidium accepted the responsibility—and frequently the blame—for them collectively.

Frol Kozlov is reported to have opened the attack on that occasion. He accused Khrushchev of being personally responsible for the circumstances in which the people of the southern town of Novocherkassk had rioted, sacking police stations, warehouses and stores, in violent protest against constant food shortages. Kozlov spoke with considerable personal bitterness, as the man whom Khrushchev had sent down to restore peace. Attempting to address an audience of Novocherkassk citizens, he was unable to make himself heard because of the booing and jeering, and had then been pelted with bottles, a flying fragment of broken glass cutting his forehead. He bluntly told Khrushchev at the next Presidium meeting after his return that he refused to accept responsibility any longer for the situation which had given rise to this insurrection, and so did his colleagues.

Khrushchev replied with a flood of abuse, and through the sheer force of his vituperation, won the day. Conveniently for Khrushchev, and perhaps partly because of him, Kozlov, who had already suffered two heart attacks, had a stroke soon afterward, which removed him permanently from the political scene.

This time, they decided, they really would be "collective leadership"—a united body of Presidium members, leading the movement to expel the First Secretary from their midst.

Two important men outside the Presidium had already given their personal support to the plot, and they were now called in to help in its execution: forty-seven-year-old Alexander Shelepin, the chairman of the Committee for Party-State Control, a body set up by Khrushchev at the end of 1962, charged with the responsibility of investigating official misbehavior in all its forms, from inefficiency to embezzlement; and the man who had succeeded him on his promotion to the new committee, as the head of the secret police, Vladimir Semichastny. For obvious reasons, their jobs were two of the most unpopular and the most powerful in the country. The two men had been associated with one another in the Young Communist League, and the nature of their present positions ensured their continued close collaboration.

The first and most obvious move to be made, with their assistance, was to cut off Khrushchev's access to any means of appealing to the public: the Central Committee and the mass media, which he had brought under his personal control by appointing his son-in-law Adzhubei to the editorship of *Izvestia*, the Government news-paper, and two other close protégés, Victor Satyukov and Mikhail Kharlamov, editor of *Pravda*, the party organ, and chairman of the All-Union Committee for Radio and Television respectively.

He had only recently demonstrated his readiness to use the press as a weapon against his colleagues in the Presidium. When he had left Moscow for Cape Pitsunda at the end of the month, right in the middle of the bitter economic dispute which had refueled the political fire that eventually consumed him, he had a meeting with the three chief communicators. Its result appeared a few days later: a fulsome description of Khrushchev's unpopular economic policy as though it had already been adopted, followed by a second one, portraying the policy favored by most of Khrushchev's colleagues in the worst possible light. They could not allow him to make a similar move on this more dramatic occasion—which, it quickly proved, he would soon attempt.

It was not, in the event, difficult to frustrate Khrushchev in this direction: Satyukov was in Paris as leader of a parliamentary delegation and Kharlamov was visiting Oslo as a guest of the Norwegian State Broadcasting Corporation. That left Adzhubei, who was by far the closest to Khrushchev of any of the three, alone in Moscow. Semichastny was able to order a careful watch on his activities in the *Izvestia* building because, like all Soviet organizations of any importance, it has its own secret police network operating independently within it.

The second precaution posed greater problems. The Central Committee could not be simply suppressed: it would have to be convened, in any case, formally to consider and accept Khrushchev's "resignation." And it seemed possible that, when it was called, it might not be so automatically acquiescent toward the perpetrators of an attempted *coup d'état* as it had been toward Khrushchev's edicts and antics in the past. Many of Khrushchev's most loyal supporters and friends were members of it and they could cause considerable commotion by demanding that his case be heard. Indeed, Khrushchev's most hopeful plan would be to demand the calling of a Central Committee meeting and then to direct the activities of his supporters within it.

In overcoming this danger, the plotters owed something to Khrushchev's own tactics in the past. In 1957, when his position was as gravely challenged as it was now, he had allies as far away as Kazakhstan and Siberia awakened in the middle of the night and flown secretly by loyal air force crews to the meeting in Moscow. The conspirators decided that they could only outmaneuver him by following his example before he himself could do so. They carefully selected a quorum of members from among the three hundred and thirty, which excluded Khrushchev's best-known and most enthusiastic supporters. By the time Khrushchev himself reached the capital, most of them had already arrived.

Khrushchev's plane landed at Venukovo, Moscow's main domestic airport, soon after 2:00 P.M. and taxied to the high-security reception building normally reserved for VIPs, away from the main terminal. In its marble hall Khrushchev had officially welcomed a succession of visitors: Fidel Castro, Wladyslaw Gomulka and Janos Kadar in the past few months alone. But today he was met himself, not by his chauffeur and his customary Zil 111 limousine (a car of such luxury and prestige that even very few ministers are allocated them), but by another car with an unfamiliar driver. His usual bodyguards were missing too, and new ones were in their places. Chief Secret Policeman Semichastny was there to greet him in person.

There was, perhaps, a certain irony in this. For Khrushchev had considered his reform of the secret police to be one of his greatest achievements. Under Stalin, through the supervision of Beria, whose brutality and sadism rivaled that of the most evil tsars, the secret police had been the personal weapon of the dictator. And when he died, it attempted to establish itself as a state within a state—an organization with unquestionable power responsible to nobody. Under Khrushchev, it had scarcely ceased to be sinister—"antisocial elements" were still shipped off to serve sentences in Siberian labor camps for political and moral offenses—but it had been at last subjected to the outside control of the party. Shelepin and later Semichastny had been chosen to run it by Khrushchev himself because he believed them to be men capable of breaking its independent power. Now, under their personal direction, it was at last proving itself loyal no longer to the despot, but to the majority of the Presidium.

At this point, reason might have forced Khrushchev to despair. But during the forty-minute drive into Moscow it is clear that he was forming a final strategy for survival.

The car swept into the capital down Kutuzovsky Prospect, the six-lane highway along which many of his most senior officials lived. It crossed the Moscow River and entered the New Arbat, named after the street Napoleon had marched down on his way to the Kremlin, and officially opened by Khrushchev on October Revolution

Day, almost exactly a year before. It went past the Manège—the old tsarist riding school, where, at an art exhibition, Khrushchev had delivered his famous outburst against abstractionism—and into the Kremlin through the gate.

The sequence of events for the next few hours is unclear. But so far as it can be established, Semichastny allowed Khrushchev to go straight to his office, overlooking Red Square, almost directly above Lenin's Mausoleum. But in the comparative privacy of this large, paneled, simply furnished room, all he gained was the knowledge that his position was still more desperate than he had imagined.

He picked up his telephone, in an attempt to contact those who might be supporting him. The private switchboard in the Kremlin—known as the *vertushka* after the primitive, cranked telephones which only the most important prerevolutionary families used to possess—automatically connects the offices and homes of the party and Government leaders with one another. A secret directory of numbers is issued to the selected subscribers, and using his copy, Khrushchev dialed his potential allies. But, time after time, he was answered by unfamiliar voices. His opponents had taken the precaution of changing all the numbers before his return from the Black Sea, ensuring that Khrushchev's office was not issued with the new directory.

In the same building—which housed the Council of Ministers (the Cabinet)—nine members of the Presidium were awaiting him. Finally, he joined them. As he walked into the room, he was even then, so far as he could see, in a stronger position than he had been in the attempted overthrow of 1957. Then, he knew that the

Presidium had already voted against his continued leadership; now he was still in doubt. Then, he was unsure of the Central Committee's loyalty; now, he had reason to believe it had been consolidated in his favor.

But there was one new factor which counted against him decisively this time: in the final analysis, he could not have lost in 1957, even if his political defeat had been total, because he had kept the support of the army, under the command of Marshal Constantin Zhukov; now, although he was not yet aware of it, the defense minister, Marshal Rodion Malinovsky, had deserted his side with the rest. The two men had been comrades on the Ukrainian front during the last war, as political commissar and artillery commander respectively, and Khrushchev had personally appointed Malinovsky minister of defense, to replace the less co-operative Marshal Zhukov. Khrushchev's purpose in making the appointment had been to effect a similar reform in the armed forces to that which he had instituted in the secret police: to strip it of its semi-independent status, and make it fully subject to the supervision of the party and the state. And, as in the case of the secret police, this policy had been so effectively carried out that now, when Khrushchev desperately needed to reverse it, it had gone too far forward for him to be able to do so.

When he entered the room in which the Presidium was meeting, Brezhnev did not give up his place at the head of the table but motioned Khrushchev to a chair at his side. According to an account given privately by a party member with a close knowledge of the events, Brezhnev told him quietly that the Presidium had decided to accept the resignation which he, Khrushchev, was about to offer them. Although they were determined that he should leave politics once and for all, they were willing to give him a magnificent public sendoff, as though he had resigned of his own accord, and to guarantee him honorable retirement so long as he promised to co-operate with them. Brezhnev proposed that Khrushchev should appear before a special public session of the Communist party's Central Committee, which would be televised, to say his official farewell to the Russian people, and to endorse if not actually nominate Brezhnev as his successor as First Secretary. But Khrushchev had said that "no political leader should relinquish his power of his own free will," and he defiantly held to this view. For a long time, Khrushchev refused to accept the inevitability of the situation, so his argument with the other members of the Presidium was prolonged. If he wished to fight on to the end, he was told, he could not be stopped; but the party, the Government, the secret police and the army were aligned against him, and the only difference it would make to his position would be that he would retire with ignominy, instead of the outward honor which could still be his if he admitted defeat. Khrushchev, as they had expected, demanded his right to put his case before the Central Committee. Its members had already been called to Moscow to formally accept his resignation, he was told. If he insisted that his colleagues prosecute him in their presence, and hear his defense, that would be done; but it would not change the ultimate result and would only serve to make his disgrace more public. Khrushchev did insist.

4

INDICTMENT
AND DEFEAT

BY THE END of Tuesday evening, within hours of the
conclusion of the Presidium meeting, a few of the most
trusted senior officials already knew of Khrushchev's
impending doom. Many more, of course, had not been
told and, in the case of newspaper editors, this caused
considerable confusion in Wednesday morning's press.
There could obviously be no announcement of Khrushchev's "resignation" until it had been formally accepted
by the Communist party's Central Committee; and the
vast majority of Russians, like everybody else in the
world, were still completely unaware of the political
upheaval in their midst. The atmosphere in Moscow was
calm; sight-seers strolled innocently through the Kremlin grounds, overlooked by the room where the Presidium met; and as usual when Khrushchev was away
from the capital—which he was still presumed to be—
the political scene seemed to be almost completely inactive.

But Wednesday, October 14, was the twentieth anniversary of the liberation of the Ukraine from the Nazis,
an event prominently commemorated in all the newspapers by means of long articles of reminiscence by the
military commanders involved, greetings to all those

who took part in the struggle, contemporary photographs of wartime heroes and devastation, and accounts of the progress which had been made in postwar reconstruction. On this anniversary in the past, the part Khrushchev had played in the war in the Ukraine, as political commissar, had always been praised and heavily underlined. School textbooks of modern history included photographs of him in the front lines conferring with generals and mingling with privates; and in the civilian areas, exhorting the munitions workers to break the even higher production targets they had been set, and touring the ruins of housing estates with words of sympathy for the homeless victims. It had been almost as though Khrushchev and not Stalin had directed the Soviet war effort—indeed, Stalin's figure had even been painted over in some of the photographs, and in others his portrait had been cut out of banners shown in street demonstrations.

On October 14, 1964, by no means everybody responsible for commemorating the victory had been told that the time had come to change the practice of the past. *Komsomolskaya Pravda,* the Young Communist League newspaper which is one of the largest and most important in Russia, was among the ignorant. General Yepishev, in a sentimental panegyric on Khrushchev published by the paper, praised the First Secretary's "personal and direct leadership" of the campaign, and gushingly recounted how, after the final rout of the Nazis from the mother soil of the Ukraine, an old peasant woman broke through the celebrating crowds, rushed up to the procession of military and civil leaders and "embraced Nikita Sergeyevich [Khrushchev] and showered him with motherly kisses."

The acting editor of its older brother, *Pravda,* in

charge during Victor Satyukov's absence in Paris, knew better. Marshal Konev wrote two thousand words commemorating the occasion, praising the party, the workers, the officers, the men and all the Ukrainian people who sacrificed themselves in the struggle. But—at least in the version which was published—he devoted not a word to Khrushchev.

Significantly, this silence was echoed in *Izvestia*—which strongly suggested that Alexei Adzhubei had already lost control of it by that time. There is certainly no evidence to support rumors—which seem to have been created in the West, on account of a misunderstanding about Soviet publishing practice—that he made a desperate attempt the next day to rush out a special issue appealing to its readers to rush to his father-in-law's support, and that he was stopped from doing so by members of the secret police awaiting him in his office.

A clue to the cause of this confusion lies in the fact that Marshal Konev, who had written the article in *Pravda,* had long been a critic of Khrushchev's defense strategy, which had been based on the assumption that any future war would be a massive nuclear exchange between the Soviet Union and the United States, with the outcome—if it could be thought of in those terms—settled almost instantaneously. Konev and many of his military colleagues favored more selective means of reprisal, of varying severity which could provide a suitable response to almost any level of attack. (This is the policy adopted by NATO on the other side of the Iron Curtain.) As a result of his criticism, Konev had been gradually frozen out of Khrushchev's inner council on defense matters and placed in reluctant semiretirement. Consequently, he was a natural ally for Brezhnev and

Kosygin and their colleagues to turn to at the moment; and this, perhaps, at least partly explains *Pravda*'s knowledgeable omission—although the acting editor, whose identity has never been revealed, must have been equally informed to have agreed to the omission of Khrushchev's name.

Komsomolskaya Pravda's humiliation was deepened by the fact that it is produced every night, simultaneously with and in the same printing plant as *Pravda*. But at the same time, their writer, the unknowing General Yepishev, was one of the last men in whom an opponent of Khrushchev would have chosen to confide. As director of political administration for the Soviet Army and Navy, he was one of the most senior members of Khrushchev's military establishment. His responsibilities as the party's watchdog in the armed forces paralleled those of Shelepin in civilian life. He had certain duties in ideological and political education, but was much more concerned with activities associated with secret police: watching for and promptly eliminating any signs of unrest or mutiny with—in the widest sense— political causes. He was also charged with preparing confidential reports on his colleagues for the party organization, and often these went straight to Khrushchev. Like the other members of the Communist party's Central Committee, he was about to become aware of the full significance of *Pravda* and *Izvestia*'s silence.

The constitutional position of the Central Committee, as the ruling body of the Communist party, exists mostly in theory. In practice, it does not convene itself, but awaits the call of the Presidium, when its formal acceptance of policy decisions is needed in order to promulgate them. The atmosphere of its sessions is recorded in one of Russia's oldest and most popular political jokes: of the secret policeman who was able to expose the presence of an American spy who had infiltrated the assembly, because he remembered Lenin's injunction that "the enemy never sleeps"—he cast his eyes along the rows of slumbering delegates until he noticed one who was actually following the speech, and promptly arrested him.

On October 14, as the hastily gathered delegates filed into the committee's headquarters on Staraya Square, they did so with an air of unusual, mystified tension. Proceedings of these meetings are regarded—like so much in the Soviet Union—as state secrets and it is possible only to gather a general impression as to what happened after the doors had closed. Remarkably, one brief account has now come from a delegate there. (He gave it to an East European politician, who passed it on to Michel Tatu, the greatly respected reporter on Communist affairs for *Le Monde*.)

He said: "Having received my summons to the meeting, I arrived to find that it was already in session. Suslov was on the platform, making a speech and, from the back of the room where I had found a seat, I heard him say: 'This man has become vain. This man has forgotten his conscience.'

"I immediately assumed that he meant Leonid Ilyichev [Khrushchev's "hatchet man" in cultural activities, who has since been demoted to a deputy foreign minister], because I had been told that his fall was imminent. But the next moment, I saw that Khrushchev was missing from his usual seat of honor, in the center of the Presidium table. He sat red-faced on a bench on one side of the hall. And so it became obvious why we had been so suddenly called to Moscow."

The meeting was one of the longest in the Central Committee's history. It took Suslov five hours to make his detailed indictment against Khrushchev, considerably expanded from the version he had read to the Presidium the day before. Reports which have since been denied by the Soviet authorities, but which nevertheless ring true, and come from a convincingly wide range of reliable sources, claimed that he accused Khrushchev on twenty-nine separate counts. Whether or not this figure is exact, a summary—covering forty pages of print —was almost immediately issued to party secretaries, to read in secret to members (who number just less than twelve million among a population of two hundred and ten million). And what appears to be a copy of this has fallen into Western hands, again through an East European intermediary. Its authenticity has been challenged, but subsequent indirect criticisms of Khrushchev published in the Soviet press—which were not known before the document in question appeared in Italy—confirm that the pattern of its argument exactly follows the official one; it is too close to reality to be based on hearsay either inside or outside the Russian borders.

It states that Suslov's first accusation was that Khrushchev had disrupted the efficient functioning of the party organization in his vain attempts to improve the economic situation. This, he told the assembled delegates, was his greatest crime—the enormity of which can only be understood if it is realized that, in the Soviet Union, the party is responsible for virtually every aspect of national life: agriculture, industry, education, housing, communications, entertainment, sport and so on.

"The principal damage done by Comrade Khrushchev's personal initiatives, particularly after 1962, was in the disorganization of the party and in his mismanagement of agricultural and industrial production," Suslov claimed.

Much of the chaos, he said, had been created in 1962, by the division of the party into two branches: one responsible for industry and the other for agriculture. (This had given rise to a Russian crack that England now had two Queens: one for industry and one for agriculture.) Its main result had been administrative chaos and widespread official confusion.

He then accused Khrushchev of deliberately undermining the authority of the Central Committee. Under Khrushchev, Suslov said, "the Central Committee was being convened in increasingly large sessions, and persons who had not been elected delegates took part in them more and more, having been personally invited by the First Secretary, as experts on questions under discussion. As a result, these meetings eventually turned into spectacular shows, and deprived members of the highest organ of the party of any real opportunity to discuss and criticize policy, or to analyze and properly examine current political problems. Indeed, strangers began to outnumber the actual members of the Central Committee.

"At these assemblies, as there was no chance for serious discussion, proposals and plans—even those of a complex technical and economic character—were adopted by acclamation, whenever the First Secretary presented them."

In the Presidium itself Khrushchev "repeatedly transgressed and violated the principle of collective leadership." Having condemned Stalin for his cult of personality, Khrushchev had created one of his own, permitting himself to be "praised excessively" in the press and often presenting group decisions as though they were his own.

This complaint was central to Suslov's case. He saw the course of Khrushchev's career as one which gradually replaced constitutional with personal government, organized through Adzhubei and his associates (although he did not name them in this context). This not only challenged established practice, but also the very position of Suslov and his colleagues, who saw the authority due to them slipping into the hands of a hostile clique. One effect of this was that a minister had tried in vain for two years to get an audience with Khrushchev! And while Khrushchev was always deeply involved in foreign policy, he increasingly ignored the advice and presence of the Foreign Ministry itself.

Having established his first principal point—Khrushchev's progress toward absolute dictatorship—he turned to its specific aspects. Most threatening of all to the life of the nation had been the agricultural chaos. Suslov made no attempt to convince his audience that Khrushchev had created the desperate situation; rather, he had inherited it, and failed to improve it.

"It is in his agricultural policy that Comrade Khrushchev has most clearly demonstrated his failure to assess problems soberly, and the impulsiveness of his ill-considered directives. In 1962, for example, Comrade Khrushchev launched a campaign to abolish the practice of rotating crops and introduce the intensive cultivation of maize to provide animal fodder. This measure was, perhaps, a suitable one for some regions, but in others it resulted in serious crop failures and the further exhaustion of already infertile soil, as well as in a deplorable confusion in agricultural administration. Then,

Khrushchev changed his mind and decided that the way to agricultural success lay in the rapid development of the fertilizer industry."

After giving a long catalogue of such agricultural disasters, Suslov turned to industry—and the bitter controversy between Khrushchev and the Presidium over the next five-year plan.

The favoritism which Khrushchev displayed toward light industry, he claimed, had already damaged steel production and resulted in a failure to develop modern techniques for the mechanization of iron ore mining. He credited Khrushchev with Russia's inability to produce pipes of sufficiently large size to link the Oriental oil fields with the refineries, and the refineries with industrial Russia and Communist Eastern Europe. These had had to be obtained from the West, an act which could easily have proved impossible, because of an embargo on them as strategic goods, inspired by the United States. This had led the West German Government in 1963 to instruct companies in the Ruhr, which had already signed contracts to supply these pipes to the Russians, to cancel them. In the end, Britain and Japan (the latter finally winning the lucrative order) announced that they would not subscribe to the ban because military considerations did not seem to justify it. But it had been a near thing, and had exposed a potentially dangerous weakness in the Soviet Union's alleged self-sufficiency, of which Khrushchev had so often boasted.

Behind this accusation were strong military as well as economic pressures. Khrushchev's policy was turning decisively against what ex-President Eisenhower once called the "military-industrial complex" in which the Soviet economy had been organized along the lines of a war machine, with a rigid list of strategic priorities concentrated in the munitions industry. Khrushchev was striving to alter these, thus challenging the most basic tenets of the industry's powerful military executive. His interference with this structure had already created large-scale disorganization, Suslov alleged. In 1957, he had ordered decentralization, giving unprecedented autonomy to regional authorities. Then, he had suddenly reversed this trend and begun to concentrate the economic power in Moscow once again, to the accompaniment of general confusion. Similarly, his frequent and unpredictable switching of capital investment from one sector of industry to another, and as often as not, back again, had led to instability and seriously slowed down economic development.

Suslov threw a series of rhetorical questions at the balding man sitting "red-faced" on a bench beneath him. Why had he ordered the construction of five-story apartment blocks in Moscow when architects and building economists said that skyscrapers would employ the strained resources of the construction industry more efficiently? Why, having loudly proclaimed the abolition of income tax—which was, in any case, purely nominal, affecting nobody but the richer members of the community, and then only marginally—had he then failed to abolish it? Why had he virtually ignored the enormous impact of scientific progress on the pattern of industrial development? Through relatively minor points like these, Suslov attempted to expose Khrushchev's character as dangerously whimsical. Now, his attack became directly personal.

Khrushchev's public behavior on many occasions during the past few years, he said, would have been outrageous for an ordinary citizen. But for the First Secretary of the Soviet Communist party it was even worse. When he took off his shoe and banged it on his desk in anger at the famous session of the United Nations General Assembly in 1960, he had disgraced the Soviet people as their representative. His temper was as intolerable as it appeared to be uncontrollable.

Suslov was on firm ground here. Khrushchev's flamboyance and even his outbursts tended to amuse foreigners. Indeed, these contributed significantly to his popularity in the West because people there decided that such human performances provided a reassuring contrast with Stalin's dark reserve. But Russians, who tend to be conservative in their own manners in the presence of strangers, were openly offended by them. Sometimes, Russians I knew in Moscow would even apologize to me with great embarrassment for their leader's most recent excess—fearing that others would conclude that their country was run not by a statesman so much as an international buffoon.

The examples Suslov was able to draw upon were many. They ranged from an impulsive statement in 1959 —which later caused Khrushchev deep humiliation—that Russia would out-produce the United States in eggs and meat within three or four years, to a claim he apparently made to a delegation of Japanese parliamentarians visiting Moscow in September, 1964. He was reported to have told them that Soviet scientists had devised a "horrifying weapon" capable of destroying all the civilizations of the world in a single explosion. The next day, after he had received reports of the foreign press's violent reaction, he complained that his remark had been mistranslated into Japanese by the interpreter from the Soviet Foreign Ministry, and thence into English. But it was a whole week before the "correct" version was published by TASS, omitting any such sensation. Suslov made it clear that he considered the original Japanese translation to be accurate—which, he said, had caused damaging "confusion" abroad—and the later version to be an edited one. In between these two incidents, he had gratuitously provoked Chinese guests into open hostility by abusing them at a dinner party he threw for them at the Kremlin in July, 1963; and crudely insulted his hosts and offended their national pride during his Scandinavian tour the next summer.

There was, Suslov pointed out, another more sinister aspect to Khrushchev's unruliness. Behind the scenes, when he was feeling generally annoyed, he had a habit of venting his anger on almost anybody who happened to be at hand. Writers who had strayed from the party line, or factory managers who had failed to fulfill the plans allotted to them, would be subjected to terrifying abuse—and, sometimes, threats of such severity that they doubted whether the spirit of Stalinism had ever been moderated.

He was also guilty, Suslov said, of suddenly springing ill-considered policy changes in his famous impromptu insertions into prepared speeches. Sometimes, it was suggested, these were announced "without prior reflection," initiated immediately afterward, and only later discovered to be impracticable—which his colleagues had allegedly realized from the start. Nepotism was a natural companion to all this, and Suslov detailed the results of Khrushchev's efforts to help his relatives: a "glamour" job in aeronautical engineering for his son, Sergei; the deputy-editorship of a mass-circulation scientific magazine for his daughter, Rada (Adzhubei's wife); a vice-presidency of the Soviet-United States Friendship Society for his wife, Nina Petrovna, and her nomination—which arrived too late in September to be processed before Khrushchev fell—as President of the Soviet Committee of Women.

In the days following October 15, many Western press commentators suggested that one of the main reasons for Khrushchev's fall was that it would enable his successors to patch up the quarrel with the Chinese. But Suslov did not lend any weight to that belief. (It was as clear to Khrushchev's opposition as it was to him that the price which Mao Tse-tung and his subordinates demanded for an end to the bitter propaganda war was beyond contemplation: an unconditional recognition that the Chinese had replaced the Russians as the leaders of the "forces for world progress," and an almost complete abrogation of its international position.) In the field of Sino-Soviet affairs, Suslov followed the consistent line of his attack: Khrushchev was not responsible for the situation, but he had aggravated it greatly by reducing the dispute to the level of personal vituperation between himself and Mao Tse-tung.

Suslov ran through Khrushchev's other major disasters in foreign affairs: the Cuban crisis, which he had provoked by allowing missiles to be sent to the island, and which he was able to end only by climbing down in the face of President Kennedy's resolve; the partial break with Rumania, which, Suslov suggested, had been caused by the inauguration of the "Friendship Pipeline" flooding the East European markets with Soviet oil, thus hitting Rumania's petroleum exports, vital to its economy, and forcing its leaders to turn to the capitalist countries in search of economic co-operation; the ostentation with which he had given military aid to India in her border war against China, which had been widely embarrassing to the Communist movement, for it revealed its self-appointed protector as favoring a bourgeois state over a socialist "motherland," and so, for other members of the bloc, created a disturbing precedent.

Adzhubei was also singled out for condemnation for his part in Khrushchev's international activities. His audience with Pope John in the Vatican during his spring visit to Rome had offended at least the militantly antireligious feelings of Communists of the older generation, and given rise to concern that he might be paving a path for Khrushchev to follow soon afterward. But his trip to West Germany, where it was well known that he was discussing the possibility of a visit by his father-in-law there as a guest of Chancellor Ludwig Erhard, created an explosive reaction at home. For reasons of tradition, and because of the memories of Russia's unimaginably tragic sufferings during the last war, Germany—whether East or West—is anathema to most Russians. To have to be the reluctant "comrades" of allegedly socialist Germans in the East was bad enough; to find the nation's leader deliberately angling for an invitation from the Soviet Union's "warmongering" archenemies in the West was nothing less than betrayal for the sake of tourism.

Suslov, near to exhaustion after his oratorical marathon, was also near to the end of his speech.

"A change of leader has become necessary because of Comrade Khrushchev's excessively personal policies, and because he has refused to honor the principle of collective leadership," he concluded, and sat down before the silent assembly.

Khrushchev was then allowed to reply. But while his speech lasted for only one hour less than the first one, he made no attempt in his defense to emulate Suslov's cold, precise argument. It was a wild, sometimes unashamedly hysterical, performance which partly served to demonstrate to the delegates the truth of Suslov's last accusation. His restraint was completely exhausted and his temper lost. Instead of refuting his opponents, he abused them in his uniquely rich style; and when he finally sat down, he was able to count on fewer votes than when he had begun.

Others followed him. Dmitri Polyansky developed Suslov's denunciation of his economic policies to still greater length, and other members of the Presidium added their own contributions, about other relevant fields. Whether any voice was raised in support of Khrushchev, we do not know. But when the vote was taken—as the subsequent official announcement tacitly admitted by omitting the customary word "unanimous" —there were still delegates who were not willing to vote him out of office. Some reports suggest that as much as one third of the Central Committee voted in his favor, and there were also said to be some abstentions on the motion "accepting his request to be relieved of his duties, in view of his advanced age and the deterioration of his health." But Khrushchev had been finally and constitutionally stripped of his title of First Secretary of the Communist party of the Soviet Union, and expelled from the Presidium of the Central Committee. Now, it only remained for a meeting of the Presidium of the Supreme Soviet (parliament) to be called behind the scenes, to accept his resignation as Chairman of the Council of Ministers. According to an East European account of this brief, private ceremony, Khrushchev had still not given up all hope. "Couldn't I just stay on as Minister of Agriculture?" he is said to have asked, provoking the only laughter to be heard in the whole course of these events. There was nothing more for him to do but to go home and rejoin his wife Nina, who had cut short her holiday in Czechoslovakia to be with him. They left for the seclusion of the countryside that night, private citizens for the first time in their adult lives.

5

BEGINNING
OF THE END

KHRUSHCHEV'S seventieth birthday was on April 17, 1964, almost exactly five months before his fall. After ten years in the Kremlin, his popularity was fading rapidly within Russia and many of his most important policies, intended to rejuvenate the country's sadly rundown economy, seemed to be little nearer to fruition than they had been when he first announced them. Nobody doubted his earlier achievements, but there was a growing, though still largely unspoken, feeling among both the public and the highest organs of the Communist party and the Government that his present defects outweighed his virtues as the head of the Soviet Union. Once or twice in the recent past he had declared himself to be "old and tired" and had commented, "I cannot go on for all time"; and if he had chosen this moment to retire—as at least some of his colleagues had hoped he would, and some of them had gently urged him to do— he could have done so honorably, instead of in the disgrace which was soon to envelop his whole career. His achievements would have been praised in the press (although other aspects of his career would almost certainly have been criticized after a decent period of time had elapsed) and he could have bowed out in at least outward triumph.

But he had clearly stated his attitude. "A political leader," he had said several times in the presence of Westerners, and no doubt more often in private, "should never relinquish his power of his own free will." And he adhered to that uncompromising philosophy until it all but destroyed him. But in April, the moment for his overthrow was not yet ripe. All twenty-five of his closest colleagues still accepted his leadership, however reluctantly, and on the seventeenth of that month, they paid him due homage.

Khrushchev was awakened early in the morning in his town house, high up on the Lenin Hills overlooking the whole city of Moscow, to receive his colleagues, who were waiting downstairs to congratulate him. He dressed, went down, smilingly received their applause and their presents, and embraced them in turn, kissing each on his cheeks three times, according to the Russian custom. Then, they drove together in procession to the Kremlin, where, amidst the tsarist grandeur of St. Catherine's Hall, they ceremoniously awarded him for the third time in his life the highest honors the Soviet state can confer: the Order of Lenin and the title of Hero of the Soviet Union.

For an event supposedly being played down, for fear of inviting odious comparisons with Stalin's seventieth birthday celebrations, when the gifts he had received were exhibited in a museum specially built for the purpose and the sky glittered with fireworks through the night, it was remarkably unreserved. All over the Soviet Union, the men who were to overthrow him twenty weeks later were seen on television praising him almost as lavishly as Stalin had been praised in his time. In a message of greetings from the party and state, he was told:

"The whole of your life, dear Nikita Sergeyevich, is an outstanding example of selfless service to the party of Lenin and the Soviet people. Under your leadership, the party has achieved an unprecedented growth in the nation's economic, ideological and political might and in the defensive power of our motherland, and it has succeeded in its efforts to advance the living standards of the people.

"Everyone deeply appreciates, Nikita Sergeyevich, your outstanding contribution to the struggle to strengthen peace, to abolish colonialism and to liberate the working class and all working peoples from social and national oppression.

"Your devotion to the welfare of our motherland and of all progressive peoples has won you the profound respect and love of the Soviet people and of the workers of the world."

Congratulations poured in from every part of the earth—the official ones alone filled two pages of the evening newspapers—and in the messages, there was no discernible note of dissidence. Western leaders praised him almost as fulsomely as their Communist colleagues; and even Mao Tse-tung (whom Khrushchev had recently called "an old galosh," a Soviet colloquialism meaning a used contraceptive) wished his outspokenly bitter enemy "long life and good health." In the West, newspapers printed their tributes as prominently as did those in Eastern Europe. *The Times* of London summed up the general attitude, discussing in its first leader "how dependent the world has become on the shrewd and jovial Nikita Sergeyevich."

It said: "The changes in the Soviet world during his administration have amounted almost to another revolution. The terror is ended, tension has relaxed, and greater resources have been devoted to consumer goods. The face of Russia has been changed. . . .

"Encouraged by Mr. Khrushchev to stand on their own feet, a new managerial class has come to the fore. These men have seen ideological obstacles swept aside in the name of expediency. . . . Of all his qualities, however, it is probably his common sense which has helped him most. His ability to abandon an unsuccessful or dangerous policy; to cut losses; drop dogma and set aside his own pride in the interests of expediency has served him well in wielding his immense power which includes a thermo-nuclear arsenal. His appreciation of the catastrophe which could follow an impetuous move has made the world a less dangerous place to live in."

Those few of his critics within Russia who have access to foreign newspapers must have been pained by this and other Western eulogies. The very qualities the West praised him for possessing—shrewdness, joviality, lack of dogmatism, expediency at the cost of his own pride, common sense and so on—they considered that he lacked. For the assumption that the Russians continued to share the West's affection and respect for Khrushchev was one of the most severe miscalculations in the interpretation of Soviet affairs since the Revolution. If his seventieth birthday was taken as an opportunity for such generous stocktaking in the West, it at the same time turned the Russians to less charitable and more private thoughts of their own. Millions in the West would probably have been shocked by a joke then sweeping through Moscow:

"Can a pig be bald?"

"I'm afraid I don't discuss politics." But the Russians laughed, fairly openly.

❉   ❉   ❉   ❉   ❉

As a rule, only the merest hints of the popular mood in Russia filter through to Westerners—even to those actually resident in Moscow. The Soviet press, of course, provides no indication of this, employing the term "Soviet people" either as a means of expressing official policy—"The Soviet people demand an immediate end to the repeated provocations of American imperialists in South Vietnam . . ." "The Soviet people applaud the heroic achievements of the Cuban revolutionaries . . ." —or as a means of exhortation—"The Soviet people are redoubling their efforts to exceed their production targets . . ." "The Soviet people indignantly reject the drunken behavior of a few remaining bourgeois elements." Employees of Western organizations—secretaries, interpreters, domestics, and so on, selected by the state agency that supplies them for their political "reliability"—would be foolish to reveal their private opinions, even if their employers were tactless enough to ask about them. And few other Russians are allowed access to the special "diplomatic blocks" of apartments in which Westerners are obliged to live as a condition of residence in the Soviet Union. Those who are are mostly Foreign Ministry officials and press commentators specializing in foreign affairs, well practiced in the art of nonrevelation and permitted by their superiors to attend cocktail parties to which they are invited within the "capitalist ghetto."

But these restrictions are only a beginning to the problems facing a Westerner who attempts to penetrate the mysteries of normal Russian life. Europeans and Americans who visit the Soviet Union casually, as tourists, often dispute that such difficulties exist, perhaps because they find the reception they are given so cordial and because they find so much relaxed good will among the Russians permitted to meet them, as well as an amiable curiosity in more casual contacts. But their compatriots living and working there find that both they and the Russians they hope to befriend are subject to fears which are no less real for being implausibly melodramatic. Officially, resident foreign correspondents are only allowed to make contact with Russians in the course of their business through the slow-moving and usually obstructive channels of the Foreign Ministry's press department and the All-Union Committee for Cultural Relations with Foreign Countries. In fact, they often bypass these but they have to do so with extreme caution, as much, if not more, to protect the people they meet as to safeguard their own positions. Through making covert excursions into Soviet society, they lay themselves open to two principal dangers: first, that of being discovered in the act, and consequently disciplined by the Foreign Ministry for "violating the regulations governing the conduct of foreign journalists accredited in the Soviet Union," which usually means a stern warning from one of the officials in the press department, the striking of one's name from the official guest list (putting the newsworthy receptions held in the Kremlin out of bounds) and in being refused facilities which might otherwise be granted to travel outside the capital and to interview people; and second, that of falling into the arms of a secret police agent who attempts either to compromise one through exploiting a sexual weakness, or to provoke one into some hostile act against the Soviet state—such as attempting to help dissident elements inside Russia to communicate with émigré groups outside —which can then be exposed in the press as a warning to others. The fears on the Russian side are greater: that if one's unofficial relationship with a Westerner is detected, one's career may suffer or, in extreme cases, that one will be summarily dispatched to contribute one's labor to the glory of socialism at the Bratsk hydroelectric scheme in Siberia or in some remote state farm in eastern Kazakhstan. It is commonly believed in the West that, under Khrushchev's liberalizing regime, Russians were removed from the terrors of deportation. But while it is undeniable that he caused millions of Stalin's victims to be released from the northern labor camps and ordered their rehabilitation into respectable society, even in the last days of his reign the labor camps were still open to receive "antisocial elements" that included prostitutes, drunkards, political troublemakers and people who had close but unauthorized contacts with Westerners. As recently as 1964, the Soviet press even boasted of this. A week before Khrushchev's birthday, the party newspaper at Klin (an industrial town about seventy miles from Moscow) had devoted a full page to a mass trial at which six hundred "jurors" had "indignantly howled down" the attempts of three locally born teen-age girls to defend themselves from the charge of consorting with Arab diplomats in order to obtain imported cosmetics. The reporter, lamenting that Soviet women were capable of "trading the dignity of their motherland for a sachet of foreign shampoo," stated with satisfaction that they had now been sent to "a distant place where such commodities are unavailable."

Most Westerners who have been assigned to Moscow have personal knowledge of similar brutality. The victims were most frequently amateur prostitutes and black marketeers attempting to buy Western clothes and phonograph records; but sometimes they were students or other equally well-meaning people, simply trying to satisfy their curiosity about the outside world from which their access was officially cut off. A conservative estimate of the numbers of such people who lost their jobs or were exiled as a result of such innocent contacts with Westerners toward the end of Khrushchev's career would be two or three hundred a year.

A student of transport economics, for example, was dismissed from his institute and drafted into the army, on the grounds that he had endangered the national security by accepting an invitation to a drink in the apartment of an American correspondent whom he had met by chance in a café; a girl was removed from the historical records department of the Institute of Marxism-Leninism when it became known that she wanted to marry an English exchange student from St. Anthony's College, Oxford, Mervyn Matthews; a medical research worker was publicly rebuked for attending a Western cocktail party to which he had been invited; a letter sorter in the post office was fired when his niece married a foreigner; and so on.

Private meetings did take place, however, and one presumes that most of these never came to the attention of the authorities. It was fairly safe to arrange to meet in a café—particularly one of those in the center of the city, where the Russian could easily be mistaken for an Intourist interpreter or official from the Ministry of Foreign Trade. If the Russian was bolder than most, he could get himself into a diplomatic block unchallenged by the police on guard duty outside, by telephoning his contact from a call box around the corner, and arranging to meet him there; uniformed policemen are never bold enough to challenge Russians who pass by them in the company of a Westerner because the checks are supposedly nonexistent. One precaution usually taken by Westerners was never openly to discuss a meeting with Russians after it had taken place for fear that gossip would eventually reach the ears of the authorities and result in reprisals.

In addition to all this, it must be remembered that any systematic collection of data about the Soviet Union—whether by stealing secret documents or reading the newspapers regularly—is held by the Soviet penal code to be espionage, punishable by sentences ranging from eight years' imprisonment to execution. Any attempt to inform a Soviet citizen about life outside its borders, except through official channels, whether by means of crude propaganda pamphlets of the type produced by some émigré groups in West Germany and the United States, or through casual and innocent conversation, is considered to be subversive. The Soviet authorities rarely employ either of these powerful weapons against foreigners, but their presence was repeatedly brought to the attention of Russians themselves through articles in the press. Several newspapers—particularly *Izvestia,* then edited by Adzhubei—also repeatedly printed articles exposing the alleged misdeeds of members of the Western community. Their scurrilousness often rivaled that of the Hollywood scandal magazines, and their purpose was more sinister: repeatedly to warn Russians that any Westerner who attempted to start a relationship with them was most likely either sexually debauched, or a drunkard, or a black marketeer, or obnoxiously rude, if not all of these; and that he was undoubtedly a "slanderer of the Soviet people" abusing their hospitality to deny the great achievements of socialism and insult its adherents. These articles were so excessive that, so far as I could make out, few Russians took them with the seriousness that was intended. ("I read in the papers about you people," a taxi driver cheerily told one correspondent. "You're just like us. When you've got nothing to do, you lie down and drink a bottle of vodka.") But they had a cumulative effect on their readers, which sometimes led otherwise good-natured people to be unreasonably suspicious of foreigners, abusing them for taking a snapshot of a local market, or an old wooden cottage, on the grounds that it would be used for propaganda about food shortages or poor housing conditions. Combined with the example set by Soviet newspaper correspondents in the West, they also did much to encourage the belief that Westerners were so ideologically committed to capitalist precepts that they were blind to what virtues Russia possessed—and this misconception was very difficult to dislodge from the mind of even the most pleasant acquaintance. So they amounted to another pressure on "bourgeois correspondents" to restrain themselves from stepping outside the social limits imposed upon them, and from exploring the life of the country in which they were living.

This brief description of the difficulties facing a correspondent with a genuine desire to report on Soviet affairs from the Soviet Union as informedly and fairly as possible does not accord with the impression many

Westerners had gained of an increasingly liberal atmosphere in Moscow during Khrushchev's reign. Much of the responsibility for this discrepancy was, however, that of the correspondents themselves. In contradiction to the journalistic principles they were supposedly upholding in a country where almost none exist, suppression of unpalatable truths about the area they covered became almost a habit. Adzhubei's attacks on Westerners in *Izvestia* were never reported to the West, according to an agreement between the members of the foreign press corps. The reasons for this were that to do so would only disseminate the already damaging libel, and encourage detractors to intensify and widen their campaign of vilification. It was held to be a matter of principle that a reader should not be expected to concern himself with the problems a reporter encounters in his efforts to collect news, but only with the news itself. But this generally commendable self-restraint has led, in the case of news from Russia, to the assumption that the general thaw in the Cold War had greatly improved the channels of communication, when it had not. It has also created, by failing to state otherwise, an impression that unofficial sources of information have become more easily available and more reliable, which is only true to a very limited extent. Many of the sources who "said such-and-such last night" were in fact other journalists who had picked up the information from somebody whose identity (for reasons already explained) he refused to disclose, and which was taken on trust. There was nothing discreditable about this practice, for it displayed a spirit of co-operation between foreign correspondents that resulted in a fuller flow of information to their respective publications in the West.

But it should not have been done secretively, because the chances of unintentional distortion are obvious with information passed by word of mouth, and the reader should have been allowed to bear them in mind.

Similarly, the much-publicized and praiseworthy abolition of official censorship of press messages transmitted from Moscow to other countries, ordered by Khrushchev in 1962, has led many people in the West to believe that correspondents there could from then onward write in a freedom comparable to that of Paris, Bonn or Tokyo. This was far from true because correspondents were now obliged, if they wished to stay on in the Soviet Union, to institute a self-censorship in place of the old official one. It was, in one way, more pernicious than the previous system: if, in the past, one had included in one's article a passage offensive to the Soviet authorities, the faceless censors working behind a green door (now symbolically bricked in) in the Central Telegraph office on Gorky Street would merely delete it before it was passed as suitable for transmission; but now, it could be sent unimpaired to one's office to appear in print the next day. If this happened once, the correspondent would be summoned to the Foreign Ministry press department to be severely criticized and warned by one of its officials (the seniority of the man conducting the interview depended on the gravity of the offense). If it happened a second time, one was almost certainly expelled and—if the Soviets were particularly angry—the bureau of the organization one represented would be compulsorily closed as well.

The areas of acute official sensitivity were numerous, but fairly clearly defined by precedent. Ideally, the authorities recommended that one should rely entirely on

information provided by TASS, the newspapers, and
Moscow Radio; in practice, one could ignore this rule
with impunity, so long as one did not attempt to contradict any of the main assertions of Soviet dogma. It
was dangerous, for example, to draw attention to the
existence of anti-Semitism in Russia and the Ukraine, or
to the discrimination against students from Africa, Asia
and Cuba, when an oft-quoted clause in the constitution
stated that racialism had been abolished; or to suggest
that there was popular opposition, whether organized
or not, to any policy the party or the Government might
decide upon, when the present system guaranteed that
"all decisions are democratically arrived at and have the
full support of the whole people"; or to report any strike
or civil disturbance, when such forms of protest theoretically exist only in capitalist states; or to claim that people belonging to some of the non-Russian nationalities
in the union (Estonian, Armenian, Uzbek and so on)
would like to be more independent of the Kremlin than
they were permitted to be, when their subservience was
allegedly voluntary.

There was one journalistic crime that surpassed all
these in the speed and the severity of the response it
provoked: that of making any reference to Khrushchev
which could in any way be interpreted as derogatory
either to his person or to his conduct of public affairs.
Once it had been committed, however justifiably or in-
advertently, there was nothing that could be done to
induce the officials to commute the automatic sentence
of immediate expulsion and the closure of one's bureau.
Few nations, of course, find it easy to tolerate foreigners
who calculatedly insult their heads of state or their respected political leaders, and if this had been the extent
of the official feeling in Russia, Western correspondents

there would not have found it an unpalatable restriction. Nor would it have been if correspondents had been expected simply to suppress their personal opinions in their reports, which most feel morally obliged to do in any case as much as is humanly possible, irrespective of where they happen to be assigned. But the restrictions were far more severe than these—so severe, in fact, that they made balanced and responsible reporting of Soviet affairs, given Khrushchev's central position in them, almost impossible.

Sometimes, the censorship one imposed on one's own work was merely irritating: one would have liked to be able to report the frequent occasions when Khrushchev used a semiobscene word or gesture to illustrate a point in public, and his audiences' often embarrassed response, but it did not seriously jeopardize one's objectivity not to do so. It was much more frustrating for the reporter—and it had graver consequences for the reader —when he felt unable to describe the more general public reaction to Khrushchev. For example, Moscow correspondents who traveled with him on his state visits to Yugoslavia in 1963 and Hungary in 1964 passed over the generally cold and indifferent reception he was accorded there, even by the carefully selected crowds organized to welcome him at factories and railway stations. The authorities in these more tolerant Communist countries would probably not have acted against them if they had done so, but revenge would almost certainly have awaited them on their return to the Soviet Union; and this caused correspondents to imply, by omission, that the visits were more successful than in fact they were.

Graver still, it was as a result of this fear of reprisal that a common impression was allowed to grow up in the West that Khrushchev's policies had at least the tacit support of the majority of Russians. Indeed, Khrushchev's subjects were often credited with an astonishing gullibility, which, it was frequently supposed, led them to believe everything they read in their own controlled press and to applaud almost anything he did with thoughtless enthusiasm. Yet the bulk of the evidence possessed by the correspondents who were molding this image of a nation led by a liberally inclined and avuncular ruler suggested the opposite. This evidence was far from conclusive because of the complete lack of political poll-taking and the obvious inability of the local press to reflect public opinion as it does elsewhere, and because it was only possible to discover occasional and often vague indications of popular feeling from one's isolated position as a member of the Western community. But through those contacts that were made, and through the perpetual exchange of information arising from these, between correspondents in their off-duty hours, a composite picture was built up during the last four years of Khrushchev's reign of a progressively disillusioned and dissatisfied population that was thoroughly tired of him.

Western tourists recounting their impressions on their return from a holiday in the Soviet Union contributed significantly to the false impression which the journalists' silence had helped to create. Students there for a short time have been particularly liable to make assertions that they were entirely free to travel where they wished and to discuss what they liked in a relaxed atmosphere with whom they liked. The first claim can be easily dismissed because few of them have ever attempted to move away from the main tourist centers, such as Moscow, Minsk, Stalingrad, Leningrad and Kiev, and if they had done so, they would have found that foreigners are forbidden access to about one third of the territory of the largest country in the world, partly for reasons of military secrecy. The second is more difficult to refute convincingly, and has often been used to contradict statements about mass discontent within Russia, such as those made here. As somebody who first visited the Soviet Union as a tourist and returned, five years later, to become a resident correspondent, I shall attempt to do so. Casual visitors to Communist countries often assume before they arrive that the people they meet there will either be specially trained propagandists in the form of tourist guides, or individuals too frightened by the thought that Big Brother may be watching them to discuss anything coherently. During their stay, they discover that the tourist guide allotted to them actually believes much of what she says. Her memories of wartime suffering—the horrors of which, even for the civilian population, were probably too great for Westerners to imagine—lend a genuine conviction to her entirely justified claim that the Soviet people's intentions in world affairs are peaceful ones. Stories her parents and grandparents may have told her about the persecutions and deprivations of tsarist Russia will have demonstrably convinced her of the undeniable superiority of the present system. The fact that she is reasonably well dressed and well fed, and that she will reject any attempt to tip her at the end of the tour, are irrefutable evidence that Russians do not live in the abject poverty which the extreme right-wing press and émigré propaganda would have the West believe.

All this amounts to an obviously unobjectionable removal of undesirable misconceptions. But, unfortunately, it often gives rise to the creation of far greater ones, because it can easily lead Western visitors to accept more spurious claims which are made to them. When he is told, for example, that although the Soviet state is atheistic, it nonetheless guarantees its citizens the right to practice religious observances without obstruction, according to the dictates of their own consciences, he is likely to conclude that tales of religious persecution are hostile inventions. And, as it is probable that he cannot speak Russian, he will not be able to discover, through reading the press, which makes no attempt to keep such things secret, that Seventh Day Adventists and Jehovah's Witnesses are proscribed as subversive organizations, that religious education—whether Christian, Jewish or Moslem—is forbidden and that Orthodox Jews are not allowed to print their own texts and prayer books. Similarly, when he realizes that, in contrast to the West, there is little evidence of basic doctrinal differences between politically conscious Russians; and when he realizes that the overwhelming majority of them believe in the inherent superiority of socialism over capitalism as unquestioningly as the ordinary Western business executive asserts the opposite, he may be led to the illogical conclusion that there is no significant opposition to the government in power. And, when people he meets casually—some of them stopping him in the middle of the street in order to engage him in conversation—express an open curiosity about conditions in his own country, he finds it difficult to believe that there is as much restriction on freedom of speech as he has been led to suppose. Residents' sensational accounts of Russians who were deported to Siberia in the time of

Khrushchev—who, he assumed, had closed the labor camps—take on the air of overdramatic propaganda; and the failure of these temporary friends to criticize the existing regime appears to be not because it would be indiscreet to do so in front of strangers, but because they have no wish to do so.

In fact, a Russian who did express opinions hostile to Khrushchev in the presence of an unknown foreigner could only have been reckless, or a professional provocateur employed by the secret police. Most resident correspondents came across people of both varieties from time to time and did their best to ignore them. It would be irresponsible to name or even indicate the sources on which those correspondents who attempted to penetrate Soviet society drew, but from my experience and that of others, they mostly shared some common characteristics. They tended to be professional people who already had some understanding and knowledge of the West, and resented the efforts of officialdom, largely through censorship, to frustrate their curiosity. Their acquaintance with Westerners would normally begin casually at some semiofficial reception organized by a cultural body, one of the societies for friendship with foreign countries, or perhaps the journalists' or film workers' union, or, more informally, as a result of the overcrowding of Moscow restaurants, which often obliged different parties to share one table. For them not to combine would have been an offense to the Russians' effusive cordiality, increased by their national pride in their hospitality toward foreigners. Conversation would start, vodka or brandy would be ordered, glasses clinked together and drained, and a feeling of companionship created in a remarkably short time. Not surprisingly, most relationships started in this way would founder soon afterward, but a small proportion survived both the misunderstandings which arise when two such fundamentally different cultures meet face to face, and the fears imposed by the political climate. But in any event, they rarely proved professionally rewarding for the Western correspondent, partly because the other party was much more interested in gaining information than he was in giving it. Also, to question a Russian too aggressively in these circumstances would give rise to suspicion that one was attempting to collect material for one of the Western intelligence services; and if he did reveal something of interest it would be unlikely that one would be able to write about it, either because it might compromise the source, or because its revelation might provoke official retaliation.

In spite of all these restraints and difficulties, I and other correspondents working in Moscow in 1963 and 1964 could not help but notice—although we were obviously not at liberty to report—that however much popular affection and esteem Khrushchev had enjoyed after he made his anti-Stalinist stand in 1956, the general feeling toward him was now souring into positive dislike and distrust. There had always been a clamor of complaint against the authorities in Moscow and no doubt—although far less is known about conditions there—in the provinces as well, on account of all the familiar deficiencies of contemporary Russian life. People grumbled bitterly about the poor housing conditions, which obliged three or four families to crowd together in a three-room apartment; the fact that the block was very likely a new one was offset by shoddy workmanship: balconies hanging precariously from the walls, pieces of masonry crumbling dangerously, ill-fitting windows and doors, bathrooms whose plumbing the plumbers had neglected to connect to the main water supply. They questioned the necessity for the repeated shortages in the shops: everyday commodities—light bulbs and writing paper, for example—disappearing from the shops for weeks on end, basic foodstuffs—fresh fish, milk, eggs, vegetables—becoming unavailable, year after year, as the bitter five-month winter began. Consumer goods, in spite of recent improvements, were still for the most part badly designed and manufactured, excessively expensive and in short supply.

There were other, more sophisticated, complaints too numerous to detail in full: the privileges accorded to party members in material things, such as housing priorities; restrictions on travel abroad, and on access to foreign publications; the pedantic insistence of many officials on observing the letter of the ideological dictates of Marxism-Leninism, even in small matters where they were clearly outmoded and obstructive; the fatuity of the press in its continued haranguing of its bored readers, and so on. Of course, none of these, whether general or detailed, was specifically Khrushchev's fault; they were troubles that he had inherited and that, at worst, he had failed to improve with sufficient speed. About many—particularly the poor living conditions—he had often expressed a determination to overcome them once and for all through campaigns personally directed by him. Indeed, much of his reputation in the West stemmed from the patent sincerity of his speeches in defense of "goulash Communism" against the more aggressive Chinese variety, which found virtue, he claimed, "in squatting in rags around a communal tin bowl containing watered soup." He was obviously pained by the continued deprivations of his own people, and he often demonstrated his sympathy and expressed his gratitude for their forbearance. But in his renowned speeches about the frilly panties, "the beauty of which the Western world could never dream," that would shower down upon Russian women under Communism, and about the wardrobes packed with a different worsted suit for every day of the week for every man, there was always a reservation that went down increasingly badly among his audiences. Because of other priorities, imposed by the need to develop heavy industry, he told them that he could not afford to let them have any of this now. They had been patient so far, and he was sure they would continue to be ready to make sacrifices for the sake of national construction.

By concentrating on these themes, Khrushchev won himself the approbation of the West, but at home he succeeded only in incurring the blame for the shortages he described. His record of keeping promises was no better than those of most politicians. Repeatedly, in his early days, he had boasted of an abundance of food which was to come within a few years. The years had passed, no abundance had materialized, and the little food that was available had shot up in price. He had talked a lot about providing more durable consumer goods. But most of them were produced in too small quantities to be available. People began to ask what they were making their sacrifices for. The revolution had taken place forty-five years before. People had been asked to abandon their personal interests in the struggle to establish socialism. They had done so. Then, there had been the war, and they had given up almost everything they had gained since the revolution to beat the Germans. Twenty years ago, the war had ended. Self-interest was denied again for the sake of national reconstruction. Now the revolutionary generation was dying away and a new one—for which their fathers had given up so much, so that they could enjoy the fulfillment of Communism—was being asked to sacrifice itself, in turn. Khrushchev had begun his rule by asking for five years' grace; now he was asking for twenty or thirty years. It was becoming too much—particularly when money that could have been spent on improving the material welfare of working people was being lavished in a spectacular fashion elsewhere. Criticism began to mount against the massive allocations for space exploration and foreign aid programs. The first space shots had been greeted with wild enthusiasm, which had been greatly increased by the astonished reaction of the rest of the world. Most Russians—and Khrushchev was no exception—have an uneasy conviction that the West looks down upon them as a crude peasant people and *Sputnik I* and Gagarin's first flight in orbit made them feel that the lie had been nailed. If it had stopped there, all would have been well. But the successive flights, each burning away at least tens of millions of rubles (a ruble is worth a little more than a dollar at the official rate) urgently needed for terrestrial projects, provoked a different response. At first, it was apathy. Soviet and Western cameramen searching the streets for the excited crowds that had celebrated previous triumphs had to do their best to assemble some themselves from the sight-seers in Red Square. In the evenings, the loudspeakers fixed to the city's lampposts blared martial music out across almost deserted streets. The point had been made already:

Russia could do it. And Russians eventually became angry when convinced that the money was now being thrown away. A cliché grew up about the achievements in space: "If they can do that, why the hell can't they provide fresh milk in the winter; answer my letter that I sent them six weeks ago; undertake a simple repair on my car; have a telephone system that works?" But it proved fruitless to protest in this way, Russian officials too readily agreed.

It was the break with China that brought the resentment against foreign aid programs to a new peak. There can be no doubt that when Mao Tse-tung won the civil war there, and the Soviet Government began pouring resources into its new Communist neighbor, many Russians were genuinely proud of this unselfish example of international comradeship, as they were later thrilled to be associated with Castro's take-over in Cuba. They built generator plants, steel furnaces, airplanes, railway engines, machine tools, emblazoned them with slogans of friendship and sent them over the border to their new allies, when they badly needed them themselves. In return, they were now being insulted and abused. Their partner in socialist construction was turning into an enemy potentially more dangerous than the United States.

Russians naturally reserved their deepest scorn for the Chinese Government itself, but they began to question why their own leaders, given this example, went on pouring money into foreign countries that might prove similarly ungrateful (they were, of course, learning the hard way that aid usually produces as much jealousy and resentment as it does gratitude). The greatest irony of this was in Eastern Europe, where people have

long felt that their Russian overlords were robbing them
of their vital national resources, and where the Russians
themselves have long felt that they were depriving
themselves in order to help Poland, Bulgaria and the
other Communist nations. But in Africa, and the Middle
East, Russians began to look for some sign of political
response to their help. At school, they had been taught
that when the captive peoples of those areas finally won
their struggle for freedom against the British and French
colonialists, they would turn immediately to socialism as
the model for their new societies. They had failed, with
a few temporary exceptions, to do so. "Why," the Russians asked, mirroring the questions of some American
senators, "if these people had not committed themselves
to the struggle for the achievement of socialism as the
Soviet party had so confidently assured its followers
they would, should the Russians continue to make sacrifices on their behalf?"

Such criticisms were generally discussed with foreigners in a muted fashion, if at all. But the intellectuals
were less reticent about discussing their complaints;
and these began to increase sharply in March, 1963.
Khrushchev had called the nation's leading creative
workers to Moscow to lecture them on recent tenden-
cies of abstractionism and liberalism they were displaying. If Khrushchev had achieved anything during his
reign, it had surely been a more enlightened and tolerant attitude on the part of the authorities toward crea-
tors and innovators. He had repeatedly mentioned the
need for intellectual freedom to expand as the Soviet
Union developed in other directions, and he had called
for the exercise of individual initiative in all fields, including the artistic one. He had once gone so far as to

praise as interesting, "though wrong," Dudintsev's novel *Not by Bread Alone,* depicting the tribulations of a lonely and defiant inventor, a novel which was the banner of the revisionists. It was widely rumored that he had personally ordered the publication of Solzhenitsyn's exposé of life in a Siberian labor camp, *One Day in the Life of Ivan Denisovich,* after reading the manuscript, which had previously been suppressed.

At a meeting of the Communist party's Central Committee in November, 1962, he had defended the anti-Stalinist theme of several current works of art. His speech on this occasion was never published, but Khrushchev told a Westerner after he had made it that "a great majority of my colleagues disagreed with me." His opposition, apparently led by Mikhail Suslov, the party's chief ideologist, heavily outvoted his proposal for more freedom of artistic expression. Khrushchev then changed course, in an attempt to defeat his opposition politically, by the expedient of carrying their own views further than they themselves would have done. On December 2, he visited an exhibition at the Manège, the old tsarist riding school near the Kremlin, where some modernistic paintings had been hung. Khrushchev indignantly railed at the artists responsible, saying that one painting was inferior to that which could be created by a monkey, and that another looked "as if it had been painted with a child's excrement instead of paint." Over the next few months, a campaign for artistic orthodoxy built up in meetings between officials and the writers and artists concerned.

At the artists' meeting in the spring of 1963, he did not have it all his own way. Yevgeny Yevtushenko, the young "pop" poet, was criticized for his work *Babii Yar,* commemorating the Jews who had been machine-gunned by Nazi storm troopers into the mass graves they had dug themselves outside Kiev. More than a hundred thousand had been murdered in this way as Ukrainians looked on passively. In reply to the anti-Semitism that persists in many parts of Russia, Yevtushenko had written:

> Let the Internationale ring out,
> When the last anti-Semite on earth is buried.
> There is no Jewish blood in mine,
> But I am hated by every anti-Semite as a Jew,
> And because of this, I am a true Russian.

The basis of the criticisms was that, as the Soviet constitution guaranteed equality to all peoples in the Soviet Union, anti-Semitism had been abolished. Yevtushenko replied that it most certainly existed, and that "we cannot advance toward Communism" until the problem had been resolved.

Khrushchev leaped from his seat and shouted angrily: "Stop it! Anti-Semitism is not a problem in the Soviet Union."

Yevtushenko stood his ground, replying: "Yes, Nikita Sergeyevich, it is a problem."

"*Nyet problyemy! Nyet problyemy!*" Khrushchev screamed back.

Nyezvestny, who had been producing uncompromisingly abstract sculptures in metal, was similarly berated by Khrushchev, to such an extent that Yekaterina Furtseva, the usually timid Minister of Culture, was moved to defend him. Yevtushenko, as yet uncowed, added that Nyezvestny might have made mistakes, but that he would surely correct them. Khrushchev replied: "A hunchback will only be straightened in the grave."

Yevtushenko stood his ground, and even increased it. "I thought, Nikita Sergeyevich, that the time had passed when the grave was considered to be a means of straightening." The audience hesitated, and then burst into applause—which Khrushchev joined in.

But Khrushchev nevertheless moved forward to his grand, final attack. Artists were to understand once and for all that, in the present circumstances of the ideological struggle between the socialist forces of progress and the capitalist and imperialist forces of reaction, they could enjoy no privileged neutrality. As much as a soldier, writers, painters, sculptors and film directors could only fight on one side or the other; and if they did not join sides with the proletariat, the party would draw the inescapable conclusion and treat them accordingly. Not even the smallest deviation from the party line was to be permissible; and that line was clearly laid down. The purpose of art was to publicize the achievements of the proletariat in a direct and immediately comprehensible fashion, and to urge progressive peoples onward toward their goal of Communism. If it did not have such a directly pragmatic function, it was to be considered decadent and must be rejected by the party on behalf of the people.

To emphasize his point still further, Khrushchev condemned the growing spirit of tolerance he had noted among cultural workers toward the West. His lauded policy of peaceful coexistence did not mean ideological tolerance, but merely that it was possible, in the short run, for the rival systems to exist side by side without actually sparking off a war. This was a point which had been almost as widely misunderstood within Russia as it had been in the West—the confusion possibly originated in Khrushchev's own mind—and its uncompromising assertion at that time came as a severe blow.

So far as popular opinion was concerned, the blow quickly rebounded against him. Yevtushenko was indeed in public disgrace as a result of his dispute with Khrushchev and the unauthorized publication of his autobiography in Paris; but this was not because he had been exposed as a sinner against the party, but rather because, in the view of his many supporters, he had been too cowardly to fight for his principles defiantly, and without accounting for the consequences to himself. As a poet, he had not been highly regarded by the critics either inside or outside the Soviet Union, but as an angry young man personifying many of the feelings and anxieties of his generation, he had attracted a huge following of teen-agers and people in their twenties who regarded him with some of the adulation their opposite numbers in the West show toward pop singers. They would pack a sports arena to hear him read his work, and the bolder he became in his statements about Russian life, the more violent—sometimes, almost hysterical —became their cheers and their demands for more. He had become a symbol for the new Russian youth trying to cut through the dogma of the past to find new excitements and new challenges.

But now he had been challenged by the representative of the older generation, and they expected a firm response. Instead, they read in their newspapers that, after Khrushchev had left the meeting, Yevtushenko had returned to recant before the old-guard officials who then controlled the Union of Writers. He apologized for his past deviations, and resolved to commit himself henceforth to uncompromising service to the party. Some rumors said that he had done so with heavy sarcasm, and had thus not given in at all. But he was next heard of at the Bratsk hydroelectric scheme in Siberia, gathering material among the construction workers to write an epic poem in their praise. The sentiment among his onetime fans in Moscow was one of barely concealed disgust.

If it is possible to pinpoint such a moment so precisely, this was the beginning of the end of Khrushchev's popularity. The new liberalization which he had heralded, to the delight of the intellectuals who had suffered more severely than most Russians had under Stalin, had now been cut short by Khrushchev himself. De-Stalinization, it seemed to them, meant that the crime of exercising freedom still remained, but that the punishment was more humane. It was small comfort to those who had entertained real hopes of reform.

6

STALIN'S CRIME

In the summer of 1963, according to a sardonic joke then current in Moscow, an inspector from the Ministry of Education visited a small village school far from the capital. In her study before she took him into the classroom, the head teacher praised the talents of her pupils, and their academic and social development, generally, but she drew his particular attention to one boy—Sergei —who, she said, far outshone all the others and would undoubtedly have a brilliant career.

"I'd very much like to talk to him," the inspector said, and Sergei was called in.

The inspector questioned him on his knowledge of geography, literature, mathematics and nature study and Sergei answered him competently, though not displaying the brilliance he had been led to expect. "Yes," the inspector concluded without much interest, "he seems to be a satisfactory pupil."

A flash of disappointment crossed the teacher's face. "He's much more than that," she protested. "He's far ahead of most children of his age."

The inspector looked at the boy with renewed curiosity. "In that case, I should like to question him alone," he said, and the teacher withdrew.

"Tell me," he asked the boy, "who is the greatest enemy of the Soviet people?"

Without hesitation, the boy replied: "Nikita Sergeyevich Khrushchev, Comrade Inspector."

The inspector was startled and immediately called the teacher in again. "You were quite right," he said. "He's most certainly ahead of his time. About a year ahead."

This story was but a pinprick in Khrushchev's reputation, but it summarized a general mood of which he was beginning to be uncomfortably aware. In his dealings with the public, his avuncular charm was slowly giving way to an unattractive petulance; and the peasantlike sympathy and companionship which he used to exude to his audiences began to retreat in the face of a hectoring, aggressive tone. During that tense summer, Khrushchev's temper finally broke not in Russia, but while he was on his state visit to Yugoslavia.

It was a momentous occasion for socialist unity at a time when it was being so gravely threatened by the Chinese. Relations between the two Governments had existed in little but name since Stalin had angrily boasted in defiance of Yugoslavia's determined independence, "If I waved my little finger, Tito would disappear." Khrushchev had set about repairing the fracture, commenting in 1956 that "Stalin waved his little finger, and thrashed all his limbs about, but Tito stayed on." His visit was to be an act of reconciliation. But Khrushchev started badly, by lecturing the Yugoslavs, on the day after his arrival, on the advantages they would enjoy if they returned to the Soviet bloc, through membership in Comecon, the Russian-inspired answer to the Common Market. For a country whose economy had been nearly wrecked only a few years ago by the abrupt withdrawal of Soviet aid and the Kremlin's unilateral cancellation of trade agreements, and saved to a large extent through assistance from the United States and other capitalist nations, it was obviously impossible to show such absolute, speedy and trusting forgiveness. Tito, for his part, behaved with impeccable cordiality throughout Khrushchev's stay, but subtly did little to put his guest at ease. His poised figure, magnificently dressed in tropical suits of white silk, contrasted with Khrushchev's perspiring sartorial clumsiness. And his attitude in general seemed to be that of an elder statesman guiding a promising but rather awkward apprentice through the complexities of protocol. Above all, Tito clearly could not resist the opportunity to show off the remarkable progress his country had made since Russia had abandoned it to its own devices. Unlike Khrushchev, who used a solitary limousine of Russian manufacture on his travels at home, Tito was followed wherever he took his visitor by a motorcade of more than twenty cars, so that he could select whichever suited his mood—a Mercedes, a Cadillac or a Lincoln perhaps—on the spur of the moment. Usually, on this tour, he selected a Rolls-Royce coupé equipped with a white telephone, a symbol of conspicuous affluence few Communist leaders have ever acquired.

As he was taken around, Khrushchev was visibly disturbed to discover how much more affluent the Yugoslavs seemed to be in comparison with his own people. On his second day in Belgrade, at a meeting with the workers of a tractor factory, he commiserated with them on account of the deprivations which socialism had made temporarily necessary, but told them that if they were patient, they would one day own suits similar to those worn by the capitalist workers that he realized they envied. Then he noticed that they were, in fact, dressed for the most part in lightweight, Italian-style worsteds which compared extremely well with capitalist clothes; but when he was told that some of them also owned locally assembled Fiat cars, he refused to believe it.

Under the heat, his irritation grew, particularly when the crowds in village after village dropped the official chant of "Khrushchev and Tito!" to shout the more familiar "Tito! Tito!" In one town—the inland port of Kotor—he stalked angrily away from the reception line of local dignitaries, and stood sulkily beside the Rolls-Royce until Tito had shaken all their hands, apparently because sufficient attention was not being paid to him.

Three days later, his temper snapped. Correspondents covering his tour had been invited to the Isle of Brijoni, Tito's well-guarded holiday home, where the two men were staying. We stood on the terrace of Khrushchev's guest house (slightly less luxurious than the one in which Tito was staying) and watched as a motor cutter swept into the landing stage from the Adriatic. Tito, in admiral's uniform, leaped nimbly off and then instructed two of the sailors to help his younger guest onto the shore. The two men walked up the steps, accepted glasses of slivovitz and exchanged toasts with us. Khrushchev seemed at that moment to be fresh and relaxed. Looking around for familiar faces, he came upon the Western correspondents who had traveled from Moscow to cover his tour and mimed an embrace, calling us his "little sputniks." But the good humor lasted for no more than ten minutes. After a series of questions, to which he had replied politely, one correspondent stepped forward and asked: "Chairman Khrushchev, how do you think the standard of living in Yugoslavia compares with that in the Soviet Union?"

He flared up. "What nationality are you?"

The correspondent replied in Russian: "I am British, Mr. Khrushchev."

"Well, you stink like a woman's arsehole. And I can tell you that's not the best part," he shouted at the astonished journalist and walked into the villa. He rarely spoke to foreign journalists when he could avoid doing so again. The correspondent concerned was eventually expelled from the Soviet Union. Khrushchev returned to Russia, and went to his villa on the Black Sea coast.

* * * * *

In Russia, it was harvest time, always a tense moment in the life of a country which has seen, within living memory, famine and mass starvation, and which has never—despite the wishful thinking of some Western propagandists—enjoyed an abundance of food, whether ruled by a tsar or a First Secretary of the Communist party. This summer the front pages of the newspapers were almost brimming over with photographs of the new season's grain pouring into the huge storage silos in the Ukraine, the Crimea and the Kuban. Headlines proclaimed the "redoubling of collective farmers' efforts" in area after area. Loyal telegrams addressed to Khrushchev and the Communist party's Central Committee poured into the Kremlin from members of rural party branches, asking for permission to increase their own production targets by as much as double the amount the state had demanded of them.

For a while it was an impressive display. Then the

rumors started. Muscovites with even the humblest pre-
tensions to affluence spend their summers away from
their urban homes, in the wooded countryside surrounding the capital, commuting to work daily—so long as the
good weather lasts—from the small wooden cottages,
which the more fortunate own themselves, and the rest
rent from their peasant owners, who move into their
woodsheds for the duration of the season. Now, the autumn was beginning, and the city dwellers were returning to their apartments. Housewives went back to the
local shops—and suddenly found that flour was almost
unobtainable, and that bread was being strictly rationed
to five pounds per day per family (almost no other food
was available). It was obvious what had happened, and
their fears were soon confirmed by letters from relatives
in the country. The harvest had failed.

Wild stories that food stocks would not last out the
winter swept the city. People began to hoard provisions
—a move which the rationing of bread had been designed to discourage. They hurriedly bought almost any
foodstuffs on which they could lay their hands—thus
creating shortages which would not have existed otherwise. The customary rudeness of Russian queues—the
bureaucratic process they have to go through to buy
anything, of queuing to find the price, queuing again to
pay for it and receive a ticket, and queuing a third time
actually to collect it does not result in courtesy among
people in a hurry—gave way to covert violence. Weaker
customers were pushed out of their places, and assistants
were bullied to produce the goods they were hiding under the counters to sell to themselves when the shops
shut.

Flour became completely unavailable to all but

foreign residents, who were still able to order limited supplies from the diplomatic counter at the GUM department store on Red Square, so long as they did so in writing on paper bearing the printed heading of their embassies or news organizations, and endorsed their signatures with their office stamps. White bread was extremely scarce: even in the privileged, upper-class area where I was living, one had to choose on many days between coarse, bitter black bread and a flaccid, yellow-colored bake of maize flour. In the provinces, the situation was much worse. White bread and flour had disappeared long ago; then fresh vegetables became unavailable; and then fresh meat. It soon became virtually impossible to find any food in the shops except for potatoes and black bread. In some industrial towns, including Mogilev, black bread ran out, and almost the whole working population came out on strike in protest. Local party officials ordered and then begged them to return, without effect. They promised to bring in food supplies as soon as possible, but they met with no response. By the time black bread was being baked and sold again, and the strikers had returned to work as a result, a whole week had passed.

In the country, supplies of animal fodder began to fail. Peasants slaughtered their livestock, rather than allow them to starve to death during the long winter. The free markets in the towns, where peasants sell the produce from their private plots, were filled with young carcasses, producing an abundance of veal, suckling pigs and baby chickens, which were usually regarded as luxuries. It was later revealed that about 40 per cent of all the pigs in the Soviet Union had been butchered that autumn, and it has been estimated that so many millions of farm animals of all types had met with the same fate that it will take at least ten years for the livestock population of Russia to grow again to its previous size.

Behind all this was the failure of the most massive, loudly heralded and extravagant project of Khrushchev's career, the Virgin Lands scheme, mentioned earlier. Inaugurating this ten years before, he had boasted that it would not only end shortages of flour, bread and fodder in Russia for all time, but that it would turn Siberia and Kazakhstan into the granaries of the whole Communist world. Hundreds of thousands of tractors, plows, seed drills and combine harvesters were requisitioned from factories all over the country and sent to the East. Huge labor forces were gathered together, of people either coerced by Young Communist League officials, or tempted in spite of the rough conditions by high wages; and the task of creating agricultural riches where no crops had been cultivated before began. In all, under Khrushchev's orders and frequent supervision, more than two hundred million acres of fallow land were plowed up. Kazakhstan, viewed from an airplane flying over it, became a seemingly endless carpet of wheat, gently waving in the breeze. But this inspiring picture faded forever only two years after it had been created. Disturbed by the plows and the cultivators, the thin layer of topsoil was blown away by strong winter winds; the weather proved to be generally too harsh and dry for cereal crops; poor varieties of seed were being sown; and there was a chronic shortage of fertilizer. By the summer of 1963, all that remained of this grandiose project, for the sake of which more promising agricultural areas elsewhere had been deprived of the supplies they needed, were hundreds of thousands of square miles of deprived, battered stalks, many of them too near the ground—many were only four or five inches above it—for their puny ears to be harvested at all. In the eyes of the public, it was a disaster from which Khrushchev, almost whatever he did, could never recover. Political jokes were no longer simply cynical. They became bitter and even vicious.

❋   ❋   ❋   ❋   ❋

In the absence of any genuine public debate over current issues, Russia's highly developed and extremely sardonic sense of humor has resulted in a tradition of political jokes which started long before the revolution, and which has survived to this day despite all the efforts of the secret police, both tsarist and Communist, to suppress it. They were sensitive material for Western correspondents to handle. *Newsweek's* man in Moscow had been expelled for attempting to cable some of the more harmless ones to New York, and I had been formally reprimanded by the Foreign Ministry for sending a bowdlerized version of one about the row with China to my newspaper in London:

"Who discovered the earth was round?"

"Our beloved leader, Nikita Sergeyevich Khrushchev. He pissed on the West and it came back from the East."

But they were nonetheless an important part of the journalist's stock in trade, because of the valuable indications they obviously provided of the public mood. Most took the form of "Radio Armenia questions and answers." Radio Armenia—which in reality takes a very different form—ran, according to the legend, a perpetual brain trust for its listeners, who were guaranteed an honest answer to any question they cared to telephone in, however obscene or politically dangerous. Some were innocuous, making fun of some of the Russians' more obvious national characteristics. A typical one was:

"Is it all right for me to make love to my neighbor's wife in the middle of Gorky Street?"

"Yes, but we do not recommend it because so many people would interrupt you to give you advice on how to do it."

But others hit harder:

"How will we be able to tell when the full state of Communism has been achieved in Russia?"

"Communism is when there's enough meat for everybody and you won't have to queue for it any more."

"Thank you. But what is meat?"

Now, ten years after Stalin's death, a new tone of anger entered into them:

"What was Stalin's greatest crime?"

"He laid in wheat stocks for only ten years."

For the first time, Khrushchev was goaded by this joke into reply and he at last revealed to his people the news, which the West had known for weeks, that he had averted famine by purchasing huge shipments of grain from Australia and Canada. In his indignant attack on his detractors, he was perhaps inspired as much by a past personal tragedy, in which his first wife, Ksenia, had starved to death after the revolution in his home town of Yuzovka, while he was away fighting the civil war as a young commissar. He contrasted Stalin's performance with his own: in parts of provincial Russia, he reminded his audience, people had starved to death as recently as 1948. Meanwhile, Molotov had been selling abroad the Russian grain which was so desperately needed at home. (Khrushchev did not go into details here, perhaps because most of the wheat had gone to Russia's new satellites in Eastern Europe.) Under the present Government, he declared, nobody had ever starved, and nobody ever would.

The sense of relief this created came mixed with new criticisms: as a result of the failure of Khrushchev's policies, hundreds of tons of bullion from the nation's hard-pressed gold reserves (the size of which is guarded as one of the most vital secrets of state) were pouring into the hands of foreign grain dealers, when it was urgently needed for the purchase of industrial plants with which to modernize Russia's heavy industry. Khrushchev, it was argued, was not so much rescuing his people from the consequences of his mistakes, but creating a chain reaction which would eventually damage the whole economy.

Khrushchev reacted more sharply still, by ordering a purge of people who persisted in telling jokes against him. Those who did so were warned that, if they persisted, they were in danger of losing their jobs. At least two students at Moscow University had their grants removed for continuing and many more must have been penalized, unknown to the Western community. After two weeks of silence, a listener was said to have telephoned Radio Armenia to ask: "Why have you gone off the air like this?"

"Comrade, we haven't gone off the air," the announcer who took the call replied. "We're just having a special series of programs for the deaf and dumb." The jokes had been stopped—but the ban itself became a joke as embarrassing as any before.

Khrushchev also embarked on a public relations campaign to improve his jaded image, reportedly on the urging of his son-in-law Alexei Adzhubei. He began to appear on television more frequently. But he was unable to relax in the barren atmosphere of the studio, and his "fireside chats" turned out to be dryly formal in content and stilted in delivery. He went on "meet the people" tours, ranging wide over Russia, visiting farms, factories and construction projects. But he probably caused as much resentment as he did good will, through his inability to restrain himself from lecturing experts on their own subjects, and workers on their own trades. He was often highly critical of their achievements and impatient with their reasoning. Verbatim reports of almost anything he said in public began to appear in the press, which had previously published only the official texts of his formal speeches. Newspapers also began to print more and larger photographs of him. But words and pictures were of little use by this stage. Russians were demanding some positive and immediate signs of change in their living conditions, which had stagnated for too long. Their leader's new awareness of public relations was of as much use to them as men and women flying in space. According to a survey conducted by the Young Communist League's Institute of Public Opinion, just over half the population were now willing to concede that their standard of living had risen at all during the past five years, and a large proportion of the sample interviewed said that it had actually gone down. Economic facts did not bear their judgments out—which made their disillusionment with the current situation all the more significant. They were simply fed up.

7

BEHIND THE FENCE

THE INFLUENCE which public opinion had over Russian politics was not great, but it existed. Khrushchev was not answerable to the electorate in the way that most Western politicians ultimately are; it was privileged merely to endorse the titles he had already won for himself. He had openly admitted on several occasions that some of his policies were distinctly unpopular with the general public, but used to explain paternally that what people wanted was not necessarily good for them. He sympathized with demands for better housing and clothing, he claimed, but he would not be acting in the long-term interest of the nation as a whole if he gave in to them immediately. And however much the public objected to his attitude, they could do little more, short of attempting to organize counterrevolution. As a result, Khrushchev's fight was not directly for public support (except as a last, futile resort when all else had failed), but against a handful of obscure figures within the elite of the Communist party. Nonetheless, the impact which public opinion had on these figures played a significant part in the struggle, because, as it turned against Khrushchev, it gave them the courage to turn openly against him as well. Whether or not a country is a democracy, it is obviously far easier—and safer—to overthrow an unpopular ruler than a popular one; and in the estimation of the men who were planning to overthrow Khrushchev, Russian public opinion had developed to the extent that it would be dangerous to flout it completely in the moves they made.

But as we have seen, the public mood of disillusion with the man who ran the country, which they felt to be an essential precondition for their action, had already been created. So the backdrop of the drama which was about to begin narrowed from the broad sweep of Russia itself to the small, secretive world where the nation's most crucial issues are fought out and policies decided in private, hidden from view both literally and figuratively by the high wooden fence that cuts off the political heart of the Kremlin from the rolling lawns and ancient cathedrals that tourists see.

Western attempts to penetrate its mysteries have developed Kremlinology into a major industry, in which —with remarkably few returns—intelligence agencies, foreign ministries, universities, educational foundations, newspapers and broadcasting corporations invest untold millions every year. At huge research centers and monitoring stations scattered across Western Europe and the United States, every paragraph, every sentence and every phrase of Soviet newspaper editorials and commentaries is dismantled and inspected for possible significance by a thousand specialists; every published list of guests at a Kremlin reception is studied to discover whether it gives any indication as to who has come into favor and who has gone out of it; photographs of Communist leaders are pored over, to see if they give any hint of a change in the order of seniority of the people in it; superficially tedious lists of slogans for May Day are dissected for evidence of a change of emphasis in party policy; and every word a Communist radio announcer says by design or by chance is recorded, transcribed and translated. The results are processed into a stream of position papers and research reports, whose importance ranges from those prepared for the President of the United States by the CIA and the less-publicized National Security Agency, to those freely distributed by Radio Free Europe's monitoring service in Munich. Little information that is sensational or immediately important is contained in those generally circulated among officials and journalists, for most of that which is available has appeared in the press before it has reached the end of the Kremlinological production line. The experts report more obscure items—"Recent Developments in Mongolia," "Political Science and Sociology in the U.S.S.R.," and "Italians Intervene in Czechoslovak Cultural Ferment," to quote three current examples from Radio Free Europe. They try also to discern general trends in Communist affairs: does the fact that General X, who is thought to be in favor of such and such a strategic policy, has had an article published on another subject in the Soviet Army newspaper, *Red Star*, suggest that his opinions are gaining ground? Does the unexplained dismissal of Comrade Y from his post of regional party secretary in the Donbas area imply that the local industry has failed to achieve the growth rate laid down for it in the plan?

Occasionally, such pedantic application produces findings of major significance: Rumania was first discovered to be breaking free from its subservience to the Kremlin from a speech of welcome to a Soviet delegation arriving at Bucharest airport. An official dwelt upon "the emphasis which the teachings of Marxism-Leninism place on heavy industry in the development of socialist economics." Its hidden defiance—overlooked by the press at the time—lay in the fact that Russia had decreed that Rumania should restrict itself to agricultural and light industrial production and accept a secondary status in the Communist economic community. But the search for such clues to Communist thinking is so persistent that, in other instances, trends have been discovered where none exist, while the obvious has been overlooked and even scorned.

Meanwhile, in embassies all over Moscow, specially trained diplomats are working their way through a mass of similar and related material. Apart from its full complement of political officers, the United States Embassy there employs a team of individual experts to study developments in particular fields, including agriculture, economics, Sino-Soviet relations and the arts. The British Embassy boasts a unique institution, the Russian Secretariat, whose five academically distinguished Sovietologists spend their days reading the latest speeches, novels, plays, magazines and TASS teleprinter transmissions. Even the Russians join in the game through the Novosti Press Agency, which floods the embassies with an unending stream of mostly obscure articles from newspapers and journals, in translation, in the two or three mimeographed "reviews" it publishes each day.

Diplomats also attribute great importance to the work they do outside their offices, although it seems to outsiders to be scarcely more rewarding. On most evenings of the year, one or another of the ambassadors holds a reception, ostensibly to mark the birthday of his country's monarch, or the anniversary of its liberation, revolution or declaration of independence. These provide most of the direct contact, except for formal business, which members of the diplomatic corps have with Russians, whom they are obliged to invite—many of the invitation cards going astray—through the protocol department of the Foreign Ministry. Primed with Scotch whisky or French champagne and provided with imported cigarettes, the Russian guests are interrogated with a transparently calculated air of casualness, which is meant to imply that the answers they give are of little concern to the diplomat, so long as they contribute to the flow of conversation. Questions are posed indirectly, as though the diplomats were seeking gossip rather than the intelligence which is their actual objective. "Have you by any chance heard any rumors about . . . ?" they inquire of men who obviously do not have to depend on rumors for their knowledge of events; or, a little more deviously, they volunteer a scrap of gossip they have already heard on some matter of interest to them, in the hope that the Russian they tell it to will be induced, at least by considerations of conversational politeness, to comment upon it, and thus reveal a little more of the truth.

Of course, most Russians of the type trusted by their own authorities to attend foreign receptions are fully conscious of the purpose of these approaches (after all, their own representatives abroad have been using similar techniques for countless years) and effectively parry most of them by the simple device of turning the question around and sending it back: "No, I haven't heard anything. Have you, perhaps? I'd be most interested to hear," they reply with a fixed smile. But from time to time, some remark is made, and the diplomat who receives it takes it promptly back to his embassy and feeds it into the Kremlinological machine. There is little chance of any such remarks going astray, because, apart from his own professional instinct, a diplomat is constrained by the supervision of his embassy over his relations with Russians, which is as strict as that of the Soviet authorities on the other side. The British Foreign Office is far from exceptional in its ruling that its employees in Moscow must obtain permission from the embassy's head of chancery for each occasion on which they plan to meet a Russian, or Russians, socially, and must make a full report of the conversation immediately after it has taken place. This has largely been inspired by reasons of security and fear of compromise, but it has an obvious significance in the present context. Ironically, it has also created a situation in which some Russians who would like to become acquainted with the Westerners, but who are undoubtedly innocent of secret police activities, are discouraged from doing so when they realize that everything they say will be reported back—a practice which has unsavory connotations to people living in the Soviet Union. Many who are willing to discuss politics with Western correspondents do their best to establish first that their remarks will not be passed on to a diplomat.

Diplomatic Sovietologists are rarely discouraged by the apparent insignificance of a remark which has come into their possession. If it has no overt meaning, then one is likely to be stuffed into it so enthusiastically that its original form becomes unrecognizable. Marshal Malinovsky once flatteringly accorded a title that was right-

fully his, of Supreme Commander of the Soviet Armed
Forces, to Khrushchev; and long after he had probably
forgotten that he had even made this polite but entirely
meaningless gesture, diplomats were discussing whether
it was a disclosure that Khrushchev had taken over direct control of the army, navy and air force, and become
his own minister of defense. As British Ambassador in
Moscow, Sir Humphrey Trevelyn, used to point out,
Kremlinology is similar to the Decca navigational system
for aircraft; instead of basing its calculations on an
actual beacon, it assumes the existence of a theoretical
one at the end of the runway, and works toward it. The
difference, which he did not elucidate, is that the Decca
system achieves its object, while the Kremlinological
one makes the people under its influence veer alarm-
ingly away from the obvious.

It is scarcely surprising that all of this vast investment
of money, talent and energy produced almost no indication that Khrushchev's colleagues were in conflict with
him, still less that his overthrow was being planned. On
the contrary, the Sovietologists of the world were united
in giving the West precisely the opposite impression,
which magnified the shock when it came. In London,
the Foreign Office had for years been discounting reports which emerged from time to time, suggesting that
the Presidium was divided, and stated that Khrushchev
showed every sign of being in firm control over its deliberations, thus defying common sense, which dictated
that, even in Russia, committees cannot possibly be
unanimous all the time, and that the weightier the decisions they have to make, the greater the inevitable
differences. In Washington, the Central Intelligence
Agency committed itself still further after months of

consultations with diplomatic and academic Sovietologists and their own experts. In a semisecret report it published only weeks before Khrushchev fell, it uncompromisingly stated that his position was at least as secure as it ever had been, and had probably been consolidated still more.

As early as 1960, one or two independently minded Sovietologists had begun to discern, and write about, the conflicts within the Presidium which eventually resulted in Khrushchev's expulsion. But theirs were lonely voices, scarcely audible in the great chorus which was claiming that Khrushchev's position was impregnable. The almost universal view was expressed in the autumn of that year in a journal published by the United States Information Service in Washington. Writing in *Problems of Communism,* Thomas Rigby, associate professor of Russian at the Australian National University, asserted as confidently as his colleagues were doing elsewhere: "I fail to understand not only how an opposition grouping whose existence is supposedly so manifest that it is apparent to foreign observers, can survive, but even how any Presidium member could be foolhardy enough to make the first move towards the formation of such a grouping.

"It seems reasonable to assume that there are frequent disagreements in Presidium discussions; that Khrushchev actively participates in these discussions and finds himself from time to time at odds with other members; and even that he occasionally gives way on matters that he regards as major issues. But it seems equally reasonable to assume that he would not tolerate any persistent posture of opposition involving basic questions on the part of any of his Presidium 'colleagues' or any sign of a recurrent configuration of opposition on the part of two or more of them. No British prime minister would, or could, fail to take steps to eliminate opposition once it assumed such forms. Is there anything in the Soviet political or social structure that makes the Soviet premier and party first secretary less able, or less willing to do so?"

Today, it is of course extremely easy to expose how totally Professor Rigby and his many colleagues who agreed with his view misinterpreted the situation they had devoted their lives to studying; and, equipped with hindsight, it is possible to discern a clear pattern of conflict within the highest ranks of the Soviet hierarchy which made Khrushchev's fall all but inevitable. It is also true that there were Kremlinologists who dissented from Professor Rigby's view at the time he expressed it. But how justified is it to criticize the diplomatic experts for their failure to understand what was happening?

Certainly, none of the journalists who view the obscurantist practices of official Kremlinologists with a derision equaled only by the suspicion with which it is reciprocated, can point to a better performance of their own. Although their self-censorship did not allow them to report as much, they were probably more aware of the ugliness of the public mood toward the end of Khrushchev's reign than the diplomats, who tend to isolate themselves more from the strange and sometimes hostile community surrounding their Western ghetto. (Some embassy officials and their wives openly admit that they have never dared to walk alone in the Moscow streets—which are safer than New York's—and that they have never ventured into a local restaurant or beer hall outside the control of Intourist, the state tourist organization.) But however strong the popular antagonism was, it obviously did not provide any indication of the activity behind the wooden fence in the Kremlin, which was the only sort that mattered. As early as July, a few embittered but apparently isolated young intellectuals took the risk of telling foreigners about what they felt to be the need to remove Khrushchev, and at least two talked of open rebellion against him. But it was drunken talk, as unrealistic as it was dangerous; and to the Westerners who heard it, it was inconceivable that similar conversations could have been taking place between Leonid Brezhnev, Alexei Kosygin and their equally embittered colleagues.

Surprisingly, correspondents were occasionally "leaked" information about political activities. Sometimes, this was apparently done deliberately, in order to inform the West of some move about which the Soviet authorities did not want to make an official announcement; and in one or two instances, the leak may have been accidental, or inspired by genuine feelings of friendship between the official and the correspondent concerned. I was involved in one such incident in the summer of 1964. In May, although the Western press corps did not then know it, Khrushchev had decided to vent his fury against Mao Tse-tung and Chou En-lai by withdrawing the Soviet diplomatic corps from Peking (the ambassador had already been in Moscow for some time) and closing the embassy there. This pointless gesture had been opposed by the Presidium so Khrushchev had decided to moderate the plan, on his own initiative, so that a token staff of two diplomats and one administrator would stay on in China. But this did nothing to overcome the basic objection that the move would not only be futile, but would achieve a level of destructiveness which both sides had studiously avoided until then, by finally raising it to an open dispute between two states rather than two Communist parties. In spite of this, Khrushchev arranged for party workers and members of the Ministry for Foreign Affairs, who would be immediately concerned with such a break, to be briefed on his decision. Propagandists were also told, and set about preparing a campaign to explain it through the press, public meetings and radio and television to the Soviet people.

I heard about it at a cocktail party I was giving in my Moscow apartment soon afterward. Halfway through, I had gone into my adjoining office to answer the telephone, to find that I had been followed in there by a Soviet official whom I knew only slightly. As I spoke on the line, he scribbled a message along the margin of an evening newspaper lying on my desk, and showed it to me. (The precaution of not speaking anything important out loud in a Westerner's apartment for fear of microphones is one which seems to be as familiar to sophisticated Russians as it is to foreign diplomats and correspondents.) I read: "We are about to break with you know who at last." I nodded. He tore the evidence from the newspaper, burned it and threw it out of the window.

For a journalist in Moscow, the use of a scoop like this—even such a plausible one—is full of potential danger, for it may be an attempt to provoke one into writing a "hostile and slanderous article against the peaceful intentions of the Soviet people" so that one's machinations can then be exposed in the Soviet press as a warning to Russian readers of the extent of the evil of which the "bourgeois scribblers" in their midst are capable.

After thinking about it for a day, I decided that the leak could not be a provocation—and could even, in this instance, have been inspired by true generosity. I quickly became convinced of my rightness: other senior officials expressed surprise to me over the quality of my sources, but criticized a few details of the story. But as time went on, the move I had so confidently predicted failed to happen. It was only months afterward that I discovered my mistake: my confidant had been a protégé of Khrushchev, and the latter had been successfully outmaneuvered.

It scarcely has to be said that there is no political reporting, in any Western sense, in the Soviet press. Newspapers in Britain and the United States devote a large proportion of their space to coverage of the processes of policy making, and portrayals of the personalities involved. In Russia their function is the entirely different one of being instruments of policy: to publicize political decisions when, and only when, they have been made in private, and to assist in their execution through propaganda and exhortation. The principle of the outward unanimity of the Government on all matters—generally known in Russia as "collective leadership"—is carried much further than it is in Western countries, to the conclusion that the characters of the individuals who make up the Government are irrelevant to its character as a corporate entity, and consequently constitute unsuitable topics for public discussion. Even politically conscious Russians have only the vaguest of concepts of the personalities of their leaders and the way in which their attitudes contrast with those of their colleagues. Few know anything at all about their private lives: whether they are married, what interests they have out-

side their work, or how they run their lives generally.
Thus, while the basic structure of Soviet Government is
fairly easy to distinguish, it is a skeleton that, in the eyes
of outside observers, whether Russian or foreign, is almost devoid of flesh.

In essence, the Soviet theory of governmental secrecy
was not much different from the British one, which for-
bids the announcement of cabinet meetings before they
have taken place, and permits the disclosure of their
determinations only to the House of Commons. But
while political reporters in London have established an
accepted place for themselves in national affairs, and are
frequently able to discover or deduce what has been
happening behind the closed doors of party and government, in Moscow there were not only no Russian political reporters, but foreigners, attempting to fulfill the
same function as they would in any other capital to
which they were assigned, found that there was almost
nowhere to turn for information; the Russian public relations man has not yet been born. The idea of "ringing
up the Kremlin" as one would telephone the White
House or 10 Downing Street to check some point, as my
newspaper sometimes asked me to do, was laughable—
even the number of its switchboard was secret, and if
one had made contact, it would only have been with
some astonished and uncommunicative operator. Members of the Foreign Ministry press department, the sole
authorized channel of communication between correspondents and Government, repeatedly invited foreign
journalists they met to submit any questions they
wished; but if one did so, one was either referred to
some statement which had already been published by
TASS or in a Russian newspaper, or told that inquiries

will have to be made, and a reply given at a later date; in the latter case, there were no known instances of the reply ever being delivered.

Yet, paradoxically, correspondents enjoyed far more direct contact with Khrushchev and his colleagues than most foreign correspondents based in London ever had with premiers and cabinet ministers there. This was simply because the full-scale reception occupied a far greater place in the official life of Moscow than it does in most other capitals. They were held in honor of visiting heads of state, and to mark the major public holidays and anniversaries, in the St. George's Hall of the Kremlin, whose marble walls bear plaques commemorating Russian victories. Khrushchev would attend them all whenever he was in Moscow.

Toward the end of the reception, when he had done his official business of exchanging toasts with the guests of honor and holding brief, sometimes curt conversations with the assembled ambassadors (on one famous occasion, he stamped with all his weight on the U.S. Ambassador's foot, to demonstrate his feelings about the U-2 spy plane incident), Khrushchev fairly frequently went up to the correspondents who had been invited (by no means all of them were—selection was partly by rota, and partly according to the tone of one's recent reports). His conversations with the press were rarely consequential: he occasionally indulged in a little joke of helping to check and compare the notes which we had taken of his speech, using his Foreign Minister, Andrei Gromyko, as interpreter, or in commenting on the nature of the publications we represented (the only English I ever heard him speak was *Life* magazine—bad"). If pressed, he would give a forceful repetition of a policy statement on international affairs which he had already made—usually warning "imperialists" not to "interfere" in the affairs of sovereign states such as Cuba and Vietnam. Once or twice, the mysteries of his future official program were partially clarified by an admission that he was going to visit a certain country. But he was never willing to discuss internal politics or the behind-the-scenes administration of the Soviet states: "You shouldn't poke your noses into other people's business," he would say sharply, and walk away. So while his comments provided newsworthy material—the very fact that he had spoken was almost worth space on the front page of newspapers abroad—he revealed little of any lasting significance.

Even if one had succeeded in penetrating the upper ranks of one of the organs of Soviet Government—the Foreign Ministry, for example—one would not have learned very much. For it was not here that the most important decisions were taken. The responsibilities of ministers themselves—such as Andrei Gromyko—did not correspond with their opposite numbers in Britain or most other Western countries, but with civil service heads, such as the permanent under-secretaries of Whitehall. And the most important Russian civil servants did not in fact work for the Government, but in the deeper recesses of the Communist party administration.

Contrary to what was commonly supposed, the party and the Government really were separate entities in Khrushchev's Russia. But the Council of Ministers, which embodied the Government, was strictly subservient to the party, and was exclusively concerned with carrying out, not originating, policies. Its work was super-

vised on all levels, by the committees which make up
the pyramid of party administration: cells in individual
offices and factories, branches, areas, regions, republics
and then the Kremlin itself. The tentacles of the powerful "apparatus" of full-time party officials stretched to
all but the lowest levels, in almost all fields of state activity, quite apart from organizing the normal functioning
of the party. Constitutionally, the supreme organ of the
Communist party was its Central Committee, consisting
of three hundred and thirty members representing all
parts of the Soviet Union, which usually meets in full
session in its Moscow headquarters once a year, and
gathers more often for special meetings to discuss specific problems—Khrushchev was planning to hold one on
agriculture at the time of his fall. The Communist
party's members—whether of the Central Committee
itself, or more humbly of local branches—were a dedi-
cated body of men and women deeply conscious of their
calling to lead their fellow countrymen toward the
achievement of a Communist society. They were often
regarded with a certain cynicism by Russians as well as
foreigners, as a privileged minority exploiting the rest of
the nation almost as shamelessly as the tsarist aristocracy
had done. Membership was undoubtedly difficult to
obtain: one had to be proposed by at least three present
members, and give evidence of a long record of outstanding political activity, an exceptional sense of responsibility in one's work and an all but immaculate
conduct of one's social and private life, and then un-
dergo a year's grueling probation. Membership was
limited to about 5 per cent of the population. But however great the privileges—priority in the allocation of
housing, access to special sanatoria on the coast, in-

creased chances of promotion within one's job or profession—the duties were sufficiently onerous to deter all but the genuinely devoted followers of Marx and Lenin from applying for admission, and took up a large part of one's spare time.

Promotion within the party did not follow the Western pattern in three important respects: first, there was no sharp division between local and national politics; second, there was none between party workers and politicians—one had to serve as the first before aspiring to the second; and third, because the Russian equivalent of Parliament, the Supreme Soviet, was a relatively insignificant body, election to it did not correspond to the sudden breakthrough in a Western politician's career when he became a member of parliament or a congressman. Above the level of the cells, party activity was dominated by professionals, most of whom began their careers as student organizers and then officials in the Young Communist League. A young politician's first appointment was usually as assistant secretary to a local party committee; from then on, his career usually zigzagged between committees of ascending importance —each covering a larger area than the previous one—and the party headquarters in the major cities. It was a progress followed by all the present Soviet leaders and, as we shall see later, by Khrushchev himself.

The peak of aspiration was election to the Presidium of the Soviet Central Committee (there were other, lesser ones in each of the republics) and few who succeeded in this did so before they were fifty. But those who did were masters of the whole country, constitutionally answerable to the Central Commitee, but in fact in virtual control of even that body. Khrushchev's supreme power stemmed from his position as First Secretary of the Communist party's Central Committee, not as Chairman of the Council of Ministers, which was the mantle he assumed in his role of an international statesman as late in his career as 1958. And it was within the Presidium that the revolt which finally overthrew him took place.

As a rule, almost nothing is known about its activities: it is a secretive body shielded from public view by the Central Committee, which is in its turn shielded by the party itself, which is protected from the curiosity of non-Communist outsiders by the Government. Its meetings are rarely publicized, and its proceedings never discussed in the press, even in the vague terms used to report the affairs of the British Cabinet. But when Khrushchev went, the walls appeared to crumble slightly for the first time and it is for this reason that it has been possible to write the previous chapters, which attempt to reconstruct the events that led to Khrushchev's present status of an old-age pensioner.

8

OUTCRY IN THE WEST

"Poor khrushchev, he has gone," remarked President
de Gaulle more truthfully than he could have realized,
when he was told the news the next day, adding with a
bow to an attendant Papal Nuncio: *"Sic transit gloria
mundi, Monseigneur."* Khrushchev had not simply been
placed in enforced retirement, but rendered officially
nonexistent from that moment. The familiar Russian
process of transforming a world-famous national figure
into an "unperson" was once again under way. Through
the previous night, workmen had been dismantling the
huge billboards erected in Khrushchev's honor all over
the capital, showing his figure standing before a background of fluttering red flags, beneath such slogans as
"Forward to the Victory of Communism!" and "Peace
to the Peoples of the World!" The smaller portraits on
the walls of offices and factories had disappeared before
the announcement had even been made.

Moscow Radio and Television services dropped any
mention of his name—or of his resignation—from their
news bulletins at lunch time. By the afternoon, shops
which had the day before been trying to sell busts, water
colors, sketches and oil paintings of Khrushchev's head

and shoulders were offering pictures of Lenin and rural and industrial landscapes instead. Books of his collected speeches were removed from the bookstores' shelves and window displays, and were so transformed from being embarrassingly slow sellers to black market commodities. Then it was noticed that the first part of the official six-volume *History of the Communist Party of the Soviet Union,* which had been published only ten days before, contained laudatory references to him; and although the main body of the text covered a period before Khrushchev's birth, that, too, was removed from sale. Even the loose-leaf diaries, which almost every Soviet official has on his desk, were changed: the page for April 17 had carried an entry noting the "71st birthday of the First Secretary of the Communist Party and the Chairman of the Council of Ministers, Comrade N. S. Khrushchev." To replace these, new leaves were hurriedly printed and distributed, showing only the date. The efforts to remove Khrushchev's traces even spread abroad: agents distributing Soviet books in the West had recently been sent an eight-volume collection of Khrushchev's speeches on agricultural policy, and now letters were mailed to them, asking them to withdraw the issue and return the books to Moscow as soon as possible.

The final seal was put on the ex-First Secretary's new status of nonexistence on Saturday, October 17, in an editorial article in *Pravda,* which sought to condemn him without mentioning his name. With all the awkwardness this exercise necessitates, it said:

"The Leninist party is an enemy of subjectivism and drifting in Communist construction. The building of castles in the air, immature conclusions, overhasty decisions and policies divorced from reality, boasting and idle talk, addiction to bureaucratic practices and refusal to take into account scientific and practical experience are alien to its principles."

Another article—passed by the internal censors for publication on the same day—was blunter in its criticisms, which made its evasiveness about whom it was criticizing all the more striking. It was addressed principally to party members and appeared in their biweekly organ *Party Life*. Things had "got out of the control of responsible authorities and party organizations," it said. "In the future, nobody must be allowed to get himself into a position in which he can claim to be all-knowing, act as though he alone is capable of doing anything, and as though the knowledge and experience of his colleagues are superfluous. On this issue, every collective must be absolutely resolute. We must learn how to restrain men who begin to act highhandedly."

To the West, not yet recovered from the initial shock of the disappearance of (as one American official put it unoriginally, but typically) the devil it knew, this campaign to eradicate all evidence of Khrushchev's presence had a sinister air, reminiscent of the days of Stalin. In London, the Foreign Office officials told journalists privately that the fall of Khrushchev could mean a return to the dark ages of the Cold War. "Diplomatic experts on the Soviet Union feared that the new regime in Moscow might be more conciliatory toward the Chinese and, consequently, less willing to negotiate with the West," Drew Middleton reported to *The New York Times* from Paris. Some NATO diplomats said that the retirement of Mr. Khrushchev should be a sign to the North Atlantic alliance that the West must establish the mixed-manned nuclear fleet as a safeguard against a new and aggressive Russia. Mr. Khrushchev's retirement, they said, was a reminder to the West that it could not always count on the willingness of a Soviet leader to negotiate. Associated Press reported from Washington: "The shakeup raises grave questions about the future of United States-Soviet relations, relations between Russia and Communist China and Soviet foreign policy generally." A United Press International dispatch from New Delhi said, "India is severely shaken by the prospect of a softening of Russia's anti-Chinese line," and Indian officials there added that the Government was worried lest the new regime in Moscow decide to cancel the military aid which Mr. Khrushchev had promised. Prices plunged on stock exchanges all over the world: in London, the share index fell by 14 points within minutes of dealings having started, and only recovered six points during the rest of the day. Most political leaders decided that silence was the most expedient course, but the Danish Prime Minister, Jens Otto Krag, probably summed up their private thoughts by commenting: "The removal of Mr. Khrushchev arouses great uncertainty in world politics."

Almost the only discordant note came from Dr. Adenauer in Bonn: "There is not the slightest cause to shed tears for Khrushchev," he said coldly. "He is a resilient man and he was a great danger to the free world."

The new leaders responded quickly to the Western unrest, by trying to reassure the major governments that they had nothing new to fear. Alexander Soldatov, the Soviet Ambassador to Britain, had been in Moscow on some unspecified mission during the struggle, and now he flew back to London. There, another new govern-

ment had come to power, by different means, on the
same day. He was one of Mr. Harold Wilson's first
callers at 10 Downing Street, and told him forcefully
that only the personnel of the Soviet Government had
changed, not its policies. It was as deeply committed as
it ever had been, he said, to peaceful coexistence, to
efforts to reduce world tension, to disarmament and to
negotiation in preference to military conflict. Ambassador Dobrynin in Washington and Ambassador Vino-
gradov in Paris paid similar calls on President Johnson
and Prime Minister Georges Pompidou, and their words
seemed to have some effect in calming local tensions,
even if they could not remove entirely the regrets and
suspicions.

Western Communists were less easily reconciled to
the new regime. Ever since Stalin's death and Khrushchev's subsequent confirmation that the tales of atrocity
they had so fervently denied on Russia's behalf were
indeed true—if not underestimations of the truth—they
had been acutely sensitive to the charge that they were
puppets of Moscow. Under Khrushchev, they had begun
to show some independence, and a new willingness to
question Soviet policy and behavior in the light of the
teachings of Marx and Lenin. It was through their protests that an anti-Semitic tract, published by the Ukrainian Academy of Sciences in Kiev, had recently been
withdrawn from sale in the Soviet Union, and criticized
in the local press. Now, the Kremlin's sinister conduct
raised far graver issues. Quite apart from their own disillusionment that such blatantly undemocratic practices
could persist in the home of the party of Lenin, they
were aware that these made a mockery of their insistence, in their own countries, that a new, liberalizing

force was sweeping Russia and that Khrushchev was a great leader of the Soviet people and of "fighters for peace and progress" throughout the world. They had been humiliated ten years previously by their Russian comrades, who had suddenly demanded that the man whom they had been faithfully upholding as one of the greatest humanitarian figures in history should now be condemned as a barbaric despot. This time, they refused to be so subservient, and openly rebelled against the Kremlin's call for another reversal, against Khrushchev. The first to react was the Italian Communist Party—with 1,600,000 members, the largest in Europe—which publicly demanded an explanation. The second largest party in the West, the French, followed with a request to the Soviet Central Committee to receive a delegation from Paris, and to discuss the changes with them. Then came a host of smaller parties, including that of Great Britain, with similar requests. The most remarkable aspect of these moves was that, for the first time, they were not made privately, but with the openness that the Russians themselves found so unpalatable. The British *Daily Worker* published letters from its readers expressing disquiet over the new situation, which were summed up by the party's General Secretary, John Gollan: "The concern among Communists and among the general public at the replacement of Comrade Khrushchev as First Secretary of the Communist Party of the Soviet Union and Chairman of the Soviet Government is widespread and deep. The great interest is an indication of the key role in world affairs occupied by the Soviet Union. So, what at first glance seems to be an exclusively Soviet affair affects us all.

"The best comment on this situation would be a bal-

anced public account of the whole matter from the
Soviet leaders themselves. There can be no doubt about
Comrade Khrushchev's great services to the Communist
cause, particularly in routing out the evils associated
with the cult of the individual, restoring socialist legality
and collective leadership, showing that war was not
fatally inevitable and the possibility of new roads to
Socialism.

"For the world Communist movement, there can be
no going back on this. On the contrary, it must be
pushed ahead with renewed vigour, energy and initiative."

He was now warming to his point: "There is now
reference to hurried decisions, lack of attention by Comrade Khrushchev to collective criticism, off-the-cuff
speeches and judgments, the use of Adzhubei as a
personal envoy, etc. All these criticisms, knowing Comrade Khrushchev's temperament, may well have been
true. . . .

"As to how the changes were made, however—this is
what is causing the greatest concern to Communists,
because of the lack of any public explanations. It may
be that such an explanation could remove the concern."

A few days later, a delegation from the British Central
Committee, together with those from other European
parties, flew to Moscow to make their representations.
They were courteously received by Mikhail Suslov and
later had talks with Brezhnev and some of his colleagues. But the explanations they were given did little
to allay their dissatisfaction with the Russians' conduct,
because they were preceded by a forceful request to
respect them as confidences between Communist leaders. As explained earlier, they returned to the West

determined to publicize their grievances and their findings in Moscow, which make up a large part of the
reconstruction in the previous chapters.

In Russia itself, Brezhnev and Kosygin were trying
hard to whip up a little popular enthusiasm for the new
regime. They had already done what they could to en-
list the loyalty of various influential factions within the
country, with greater apparent success than their efforts
had enjoyed among Communists abroad. In a series of
special messages addressed to these groups, intellectuals
were promised that the policy of peaceful coexistence
would continue and that they had no cause to fear any
new wave of Stalinist oppression within the arts; senior
military officers were told that Khrushchev's basic military strategy would be reversed (he had argued, to their
strong objections, that preparations for massive retaliation in response to attack were not only cheaper, but
more effective deterrents than the system of a series of
graduated responses which they favored); and, perhaps
most important, industrial managers and planners were
told that a major reform of the economic organization
of the country would be instituted with the utmost urgency, incorporating the wide use of the profit motive,
and giving a large sector of light industry the autonomy
for which it had pleaded for so long, on grounds of
efficiency.

Turning their attention to the general public, they
showed an unprecedented concern for popular opinion.
They made no major concessions, but they did hand out
a series of minor yet significant luxuries. First, they
ordered that huge shipments of flour be brought into the
larger cities and distributed to housewives at the rate

of five pounds for each family. It was the first flour to be seen in Moscow shops for more than a year and for a still longer period in the provinces, and it arrived in good time for the traditional Russian pasties and cakes to be baked in time for the Revolution Day celebrations on November 7. Then, restaurants in city centers were ordered to stay open to customers until one o'clock every morning. This had been the practice under Stalin, but Khrushchev had told them to close their doors at 11:00 P.M. because, he explained, people who went to bed much later than that would not be fit for a full day's socialist labor the next morning. The irritation this new extension removed was a small one, but it did at least mean that for the first time in years one could go to the theater or the movies for an evening performance, and still be able to get a meal afterward. (Many were the tourists in the days of Khrushchev who went to bed hungry, because they had not been warned of the necessity of eating *before* going to the Bolshoi.) A decree was rushed out, extending the New Year's holidays from two to three days on full pay for every Soviet worker. This was, perhaps, the most popular move of all, because public holidays in Russia are celebrated far more thoroughly and sometimes wildly than they are in most countries. Weeks are spent in preparations, and parties have often been known to continue for several days. This decree was followed soon afterward by another, stating that Victory in Europe Day and International Women's Day would henceforth be full public holidays as well.

The message all this was intended to convey was that from now on, the party and Government would pay proper attention to the feelings of the masses, and that it was no longer un-Communist to enjoy oneself. But the populace scarcely stirred in response to this belated arrival of public relations.

9

REVOLT IN THE EAST

THE OPEN indifference with which Russians in Moscow received the news, when it was finally announced on Friday morning of the sixteenth, shocked Westerners who witnessed it almost as much as the mass hysteria that had followed Stalin's death almost eleven years before. Then, in spite of the suspension of public transport services going into the capital, and the barricades sealing off the center from the suburbs, people had poured in from the countryside and huge crowds had stampeded down the main streets to the Hall of Columns, where the dictator's body was lying in state. At least hundreds of people had been trampled and crushed to death in the gutters and against walls, lampposts and the armored sides of riot trucks. Now, the life of the city continued with an unnerving normality. While the West stood still, tensely watching for the first sign of the way the new political wind was blowing, Russians glanced at the brief statement in the morning newspapers (the evening ones did not trouble to carry it) and went to work. Foreign correspondents touring the city in search of the smallest reaction found none—although one did find two old ladies window-shopping outside GUM in Red

Square who said that they had not yet heard the news. Some thought that there were a few more policemen on duty, but others were unsure.

The West was mourning the political demise of a great statesman who had helped to consolidate world peace and who had turned Communism into a force with which for the first time in its history it seemed possible—if still often troublesome—to live. Throughout the world, there were fears of what might come after him; but few of Khrushchev's fellow countrymen (excepting, presumably, his own family circle) shed any tears for his passing, or appeared any more concerned as to what was to happen now that he had gone than they had been when he was still in power. Rarely has a people so clearly demonstrated the attitude of *plus ça change, plus c'est la même chose:* they knew almost as little as people outside the Soviet Union about the two men who had succeeded him, but saw no reason to believe that their policies would be substantially different. They showed little sign either of regretting that one era was ended, or of paying more than a momentary thought to the new. The closest most of them had come to political reality was watching the large black limousines speed to and from the Kremlin along the lanes reserved for them down the centers of the streets, with a party leader hidden from public view in the curtained rear compartment. The characters and individual opinions of these men are said to be irrelevant to their conduct of party affairs, so they are never discussed in the press and, as a result, they never assume any recognizably human form in the eyes of the majority. They are just there, and to most Russians there is no point in taking the matter further. "What they do doesn't concern us. It's nothing but a fuss," a Russian sailor told West German reporters when he was on shore leave soon afterward; "Khrushchev's dismissal was unexpected, but it isn't very significant," added a young teacher from Kazakhstan. "People aren't much interested in politics. They are preoccupied with their personal affairs."

James Reston, visiting Moscow for *The New York Times,* was not alone in concluding that the Russian attitude was one of cynicism. But there was good reason to believe that, so far as the younger, better educated Russians—including a number of officials—are concerned, this judgment was far from fair. For many of them refused, on this occasion, to show the same restraint as their elders did in questioning the apparent discrepancy between the tenets of Marxism-Leninism that they had been brought up to believe, and the conduct of the politicians who were supposed to be remolding the Soviet state according to its dictates. If Russia was now ruled, as they had been repeatedly told, by the "dictatorship *of* the proletariat" (replacing the tsarist dictatorship *over* the proletariat), why were the workings of the Government at such critical times as this so completely concealed from the proletariat? If the men in the Kremlin were the "representatives of the working classes," why did they not hold themselves answerable to the working classes?

A remarkable demonstration of this attitude came in private reports from Leningrad. There, it was said, a group of students marched down the long corridors of the university, holding up placards stating: "We want to know the truth," and demanding a meeting with the rector. When he saw them, he apparently heard their case and assured them that they would be given a full account of the events in Moscow "at the earliest possible opportunity." But, judging from the continued complaints of young intellectuals elsewhere in Russia, they have yet to receive the promised explanation.

Neither they nor their contemporaries in other parts of the country were protesting against Khrushchev's dismissal as such; but they were protesting that the very progress toward civilized politics which they hoped would result from it had immediately been denied by the sinister, secretive way in which it had been achieved, as though in imitation of the methods Khrushchev himself had used to dispose of his predecessors. Khrushchev, in their opinion, had been the best of the Stalinist generation of politicians they could have had as their leader; but the new men were essentially not Stalinists, and more democratic standards were expected of them. "Khrushchev failed to establish socialist democracy," an official told Westerners at a reception in Moscow soon afterward, "and so he was replaced." But another official said more privately: "None of us likes the way in which it was done. There are a lot of questions that should be answered." Radio Armenia's comment came in the form of an untranslatable pun. "How are we going to live now that we have democratic rule?" a listener allegedly asked. *"Po-brezhnemu,"* the chairman of the brain trust replied, which means both "as before" and "according to Brezhnev."

If the voices of dissent were lonely ones inside Russia, outside its borders they resounded throughout the Communist world, astonishing the Western Kremlinologists as deeply as the apparent domestic calm. In the first days of their power, Leonid Brezhnev and Alexei Kosygin found themselves greeted, particularly from the

Soviet Union's onetime colonies in Eastern Europe, by an unprecedentedly loud chorus of protest, instead of the straightforward messages of approval and loyalty they appear to have been counting upon. Only the Rumanians remained silent, to demonstrate their indifference to Soviet affairs. The once cautious Poles, grateful Hungarians and abjectly obedient East Germans now refused to maintain the obedient silence expected of them. They were not protesting against the change of power as such, or challenging the two new leaders' right to replace Khrushchev, or demanding any veto in the internal affairs of Soviet politics. But they refused to accept the Kremlin's fiction that if one publicly ignored Khrushchev, popular memory of him would go away, and the embarrassed hope of the new leadership that it would do so as soon as possible. They were refusing to rewrite the history of the Soviet bloc, in fact, to suit the convenience of the new regime. But first, before the protests, there was fear and confusion, which plunged this great area from Berlin in the northeast to Sofia in the southwest into a gloom which recalled the Stalin era.

"The announcement of Khrushchev's removal was made on October 15, it is now October 19, and the mental and political confusion is still apparent for all to see," Radio Free Europe's research center reported from Munich, with ill-concealed satisfaction. Janos Kadar, the Hungarian leader, was on a state visit to Poland when it happened. On that Thursday the 15th, his host Wladyslaw Gomulka was showing him around a new steel mill outside Warsaw, followed a few paces behind by a group of Polish and foreign journalists that included Joseph Smith, who was then the Warsaw correspondent for United Press International. When the tour was about half completed, at a few minutes past one o'clock, Smith saw an official come up to Gomulka and take him to one side. Gomulka left the factory floor, went into a nearby office and picked up a telephone. A few minutes later he returned, asked the director of the plant for the use of his office, and took Kadar to it. They stayed there for half an hour before re-emerging, and then drove immediately back to Warsaw. None of the journalists left behind in the factory knew what had happened, and were unable to find out; but the situation was obviously tense.

Kadar and Gomulka seem to have passed the afternoon alone together, in the latter's office. According to unofficial Polish accounts of their talks up to that point, they had been largely concerned with the future relations of their two countries with Moscow, in the context of the Sino-Soviet dispute. The two men were already in disagreement, and the new situation increased their differences. Kadar had been arguing that they should commit themselves unreservedly to Russia's stand against the Chinese, who, he believed, had persuaded Khrushchev to employ the armed brutality he did to suppress the Hungarian uprising of 1956 by the Chinese suggestion that otherwise the Marxist-Leninist movement would be betrayed by Russia. And so long as the Russians felt the need to answer Chinese accusations of "softness" in the struggle against the forces of imperialism and reaction, he said, they would be less liberal than their own inclinations would lead them to be. Gomulka held that at least in the short term, the dispute was to the advantage of the Soviet bloc countries of Eastern Europe, because it made the Russians feel the need to be more considerate in their relations with them for fear of losing their support in the ideological conflict. He did not suggest that the East Europeans should attempt to play the great Communist powers against each other (although the Rumanians had recently done so with considerable success), but that the situation should be exploited, by making it clear that loyalty to Moscow was no longer automatic or unquestioning. What was to be done now? It was likely that Khrushchev's wild mishandling of the dispute was one of the causes of his overthrow, and that Brezhnev and Kosygin would attempt to improve relations again with Peking. This could lead them to adopt a less conciliatory attitude toward the liberalizing governments of Eastern Europe, and particularly the growing independence in their relations with Western countries, on which their economy was increasingly dependent. Should they unequivocally offer their support to the new men in the Kremlin, and avoid any possible beginning to a showdown, or should they withhold it temporarily, in the hope of gaining new concessions? For the time being, they apparently agreed to do nothing.

Radio Moscow broke the news to its Polish listeners in a Polish-language transmission beamed to Warsaw at 10:20 that Thursday evening, and Radio Warsaw followed twenty minutes later. Gomulka had good reason to delay the announcement for as long as possible, for the sake of his own increasingly vulnerable position. When he had come to power in 1956, not long out of jail, where he had been imprisoned for "Titoist deviation," he had been jubilantly acclaimed as a liberalizer who was to help the Poles to regain their individual freedoms, and a nationalist who would win for his country a newly independent status within the Soviet bloc. (However much the Poles disliked the Russians, few

wanted to break with Moscow completely—they feared
the Germans too much for that.) But since then, economic stagnation leading to repeated food shortages and
disillusionment over the sincerity of the new regime's
liberal pronouncements had soured Gomulka's original
popularity. A new wave of intellectual defiance—reflected in such cynical comments to foreigners as: "I'm
not a Catholic, but I have to attend Mass to show I'm
not a Communist," and: "I was accused of being a revi-
sionist, but I told them I couldn't be because I hadn't
believed in Marxism-Leninism in the first place"—led
Gomulka to take repressive measures, which only served
to worsen his position still further. One Warsaw intellectual summed up the situation: "Gomulka used to be
a Communist who behaved like a Pole. Now he's a Pole
behaving like a Communist." Gomulka's authority was
deliberately challenged in the summer of 1964 by a
group of distinguished writers and artists, and with
seeming reluctance he had one of them sentenced to a
token prison term for contributing to anti-Communist
propaganda organs in the West, including Radio Free
Europe and the *Polish Daily* in Britain. He quickly discovered the truth of the Polish saying that "martyrdom
is the semen of dissent." The Union of Writers was in
uproar and the students of Warsaw and Krakow Universities were organizing student demonstrations.

Gomulka's career and reputation had been closely tied
to Khrushchev's, initially because it was the latter who
had enabled him to come to power, and subsequently
because of the intimate political and personal relationship which had developed between them at their
frequent meetings. Khrushchev was known to have repeatedly gone to a hunting lodge in the Polish forests

just south of the Russian border, to consult with him on matters which ranged far wider than Soviet-Polish affairs. As the personification of their Soviet overlords, Khrushchev was by no means entirely popular among the Poles at that moment: on his last state visit to Warsaw, at the end of July, 1964, the crowds that had wildly cheered and almost crushed Senator Robert Kennedy and his family on an unannounced private visit a few months before stood in glum silence in the places allotted to them. Now that Khrushchev had gone, it seemed possible that some Poles might try to use the confusion to remove his ally, Gomulka, at the same time.

The sale of vodka was immediately prohibited, and the liquor stores closed. Policemen toured the night clubs and "twist bars," ordering their managers to close by 1:00 A.M.—two hours earlier than usual. A young military doctor in Warsaw was awakened by military policemen knocking at his door and told that he was under orders to report immediately to the local army barracks. Fearing that there had been some accident, he arrived there to find nothing but chaos caused by bleary-eyed officers pouring in from all over the neighborhood, and told to stand by for further instructions —which finally came late the next morning, when they were allowed to disband and return home as discreetly as they could. The Government had apparently decided to adopt a calmer approach than that signified by a military alert.

One of the main fears of the Poles, who are staunchly pro-Western outside their official activities and like to describe themselves as the "West Europeans of the Soviet bloc," was that Brezhnev and Kosygin might allow East-West relations to refreeze, in their eagerness to compromise with the Chinese. On Friday the sixteenth, Gomulka and his Prime Minister, Jozef Cyrankiewicz, communicated this anxiety to Moscow in a message of greetings, offering "heartfelt wishes for success in the task of strengthening world peace." But the next evening, Gomulka adopted a blander tone, as though the event could be considered as a routine move, which would affect nothing outside the Soviet borders and little within it. At the mass rally marking the end of Kadar's stay, he tried to reassure his audience by stating with calculated self-assurance:

"The changes have come, perhaps, as a surprise to many people. But I have not been surprised personally by the news. I hope that I shall not commit an indiscretion if I say now that Comrade Khrushchev, in a talk with me in the autumn of last year, told me that he was considering the possibility of resigning from all his positions."

He was equally reassuring about Khrushchev's successors: "We have had frequent opportunity to ascertain their fraternal attitude to our country. Maybe not everybody is aware of it—although it has been mentioned in the press—but Comrade Brezhnev's brother, a specialist in metallurgical engineering, has worked for a long time at the Lenin Foundry here, helping our specialists, our working class, in assembling the plant and in the effective operation of this great combine."

Janos Kadar listened in silence to his host's attempt to allay the dark fears of his audience with these cozy irrelevancies, which, not surprisingly, had the opposite effect to that which was intended. Later that night, he and his party left in their special train for Budapest, where, when they arrived the next morning, they were welcomed home by the whole Politburo (excluding one member who was ill at the time) and a crowd of several thousand workers who had been given time off from their factories for the occasion. Standing on a dais erected in the station's porchway, Kadar spoke for some time about the talks he had had with Gomulka on the "regrettable divergency of views in the international Communist movement." Then he paused, and his habitually monotonous tone suddenly changed to one of a compelling, almost vehement vivacity in total contrast to Gomulka's of the evening before. "I want to refer to one event which happened during our absence, and which surprised us." He paused again. "This I want to state sincerely and honestly." He paused a third time, and then said:

"I think that Comrade Khrushchev showed great qualities in his struggle against the Stalinist personality cult and in his efforts to maintain peace. The hundreds of thousands of Hungarians who greeted Khrushchev in the recent past and also this year in Hungary—and I know they did so from their hearts—as the representative of the great Soviet party and state and people, as well as the indefatigable fighter for peace, were right to do so. There is no cause to have regrets about this."

When the applause—which far exceeded anything demanded by Communist etiquette—finally began to die down, he continued more quietly, but with equal firmness: "What is important for you to know now is that the stand of the Hungarian Government on all important issues—peace, peaceful coexistence, the unity of the socialist camp and the problems facing the international workers' movement—has not changed one iota and will not change in the future."

Then, returning to his normal tone, he concluded by assuring his audience that Brezhnev and Kosygin were known to be friends of Hungary, and were known to support and to have helped in the shaping of Soviet policy under Khrushchev, which they had now assured him would continue without change.

While he was still in Warsaw, Kadar had already laid down a similar line for Hungarian party officials to follow in the press and in their dealings with the public. On Thursday night, as elsewhere in Eastern Europe, Budapest Radio gave listeners to its midnight newscast only the brief announcement from Moscow, that Khrushchev had "asked to be relieved of his duties in view of his advanced age and the deteriorating condition of his health," without comment or explanation. The next morning—according to an account given by a woman employee of the radio station, which is worth repeating because it probably characterized the general reaction in Hungary—the staff arrived for work on time, but showing signs of sleeplessness and strain. Conversation between them was perfunctory, and did not include the previous evening's news, which was now being broadcast in special bulletins in the program breaks together with brief biographies of Brezhnev and Kosygin. At about 10:00 A.M. our informant went into the lavatory, and heard sobbing coming from behind the locked door of one of the cubicles.

"What's the matter?" she shouted above the door. The sobbing continued. She tapped on the door and tried again, more gently: "Why don't you come out and tell me what's the matter? Please."

The door opened, and a girl scarcely old enough to remember Stalin and probably too young to have taken part in the revolt of 1956, emerged shaking. "What happens if they start doing it to us again?" she asked hysterically. "What shall we do? I don't think I'll be able to stand it."

They talked for a while, but hardly reassuringly, and went back to their offices to try to reapply themselves to their work.

In the afternoon, the secretary of the station's party cell called a meeting, having at last received instructions. "Comrades, what is the matter with you all?" he demanded. "Why are you all so nervous and hysterical? Why on earth don't you talk to each other about what's happened? These aren't Stalin's times. Pull yourselves together."

It was the first relief from the day's tensions, and they began to do so.

Budapest Radio broadcast its first commentary on the change at eight o'clock that evening, and it unreservedly praised Khrushchev as "a great fighter for peace, peaceful coexistence and disarmament." The next morning, *Pravda* published its editorial accusing Khrushchev without naming him of "building castles in the air, immature conclusions, hasty decisions," and so on, but stating that the Soviet party and Government would continue the same policies as in the past; Budapest Radio repeated the assurances but omitted the criticisms.

The East German Communists reacted with less decision but—given the added subservience of their position, which is dictated by the refusal of almost all countries outside the Soviet bloc to recognize the existence of their state—with an almost equal defiance of the Kremlin's wish to have Khrushchev removed overnight from the annals of Soviet history. Their Government news agency, ADN, was the first in Eastern Europe to report the news, which was followed in Berlin by forty-eight hours of official silence, except for the transmission of formal messages to the new leaders in Moscow. But, during this time, Walter Ulbricht had been no less disturbed, and at least as active as any of his colleagues elsewhere in the bloc. He called in Soviet Ambassador Abrasimov, to demand a full explanation, and then convened a meeting of the East German Politburo to "consider the decisions of the Central Committee of the Communist party on October 14."

Although *Pravda* had clearly laid down the Soviet line that Khrushchev had become an "unperson," through the lengths it went to avoid mention of his name in its attack on him, Ulbricht and his colleagues prepared a communiqué which stated: "The news of Comrade N. S. Khrushchev's release from his functions has given rise to deep emotion in our party and among our people. It is well known that Comrade Khrushchev displayed considerable merits in implementing the Marxist-Leninist policies worked out by the Central Committee of the Soviet Communist Party." And they disassociated themselves from the official criticisms by assuming that "the Plenum of the Central Committee has obviously made these decisions because Comrade Khrushchev showed himself to be no longer equal to his tasks"—the operative words being "no longer." In conclusion, they offered Brezhnev and Kosygin congratulations with a pious reminder of their own position that "we shall work together, so that the Treaty of Friendship, Mutual Support and Co-operation between the German Democratic

Republic and the U.S.S.R. will be honorably carried out."

Unlike some of his neighbors, Antonín Novotný, the Czech President and party leader, was more concerned to reassure his own restless population than he was to defy, rebuke or lecture Moscow on its methods of disposing of unwanted politicians or its future policies. The nation's newspapers and radio stations concentrated on relaying comment from the West—including President Johnson's televised statement that the United States did not intend to alter its policies toward the Soviet Union —and from other Communist countries, selected to give the impression that all was still well with the world. When the Czechs were given the official reaction of their Government, it turned out to be remarkably timid, going so far as to accept the explanation—which the Russians had themselves tacitly denied within a day of publicizing it—that Khrushchev had resigned for reasons of health. The nearest Czechoslovakia came to the truth was in the Young Communist League paper, which complacently told its readers: "Great people are said to know when to depart. We doubt whether Nikita S. Khrushchev attached any great importance to this art. Nevertheless, there could not have been a more dignified conclusion to the term of his beneficent work at the head of the U.S.S.R. than the triumphant space flight of *Voskhod.*"

The Bulgarian Communists, in their efforts to maintain their party's record as the only one which remains unwaveringly loyal to Moscow, whatever the latter may do, went further. They went so far, in fact, that they exceeded the terms of the statement with which they had hurriedly agreed. The Russians had never claimed, but had implied otherwise, that Khrushchev's resignation had been accepted unanimously by the Central Committee, yet the Bulgarian Communist party in an official announcement expressed "its conviction that the decisions in Moscow were taken unanimously." They seemed to be underestimating themselves when, in another part of the statement, they said: "The Bulgarian Communist party has always marched, and will in the future march, side by side, with unflinching unity, with the great party of Lenin," for, in their enthusiasm to keep up with their brothers, they were apparently marching more quickly.

Bulgaria is an exception among the Communist countries of Eastern Europe, in that it has no anti-Russian tradition. On the contrary, the two peoples are closely allied through their similar languages and their closely connected cultural and social traditions. Twice, Russia has freed Bulgaria from outside oppression—once, in the 1870s from the Turks, and again, in 1944 and 1945, from the Nazis; and the Bulgarians are undoubtedly grateful for these salvations. Under Khrushchev, as the other countries in the Soviet bloc gradually loosened their bonds with the Kremlin—or, in the case of Albania, violently severed them—Bulgaria never moved forward from its policy of following the Russians in almost everything, whether it concerned domestic or foreign affairs.

Bulgaria's total dependence on the Soviet Union was reflected in its trade statistics, which showed that more than half its exports were bought by the Soviet Union, and almost all the capital invested in industry since the war had been provided in the form of long-term, low-interest loans, machinery and plants, and outright gifts. Now, the Bulgarian leader, Todor Zhivkov, pledged the situation would continue as it had been. But later, dramatic events in Sofia, the capital, have shown that he gravely miscalculated the mood of his people. A spirit of independence was stirring, which, in the spring of 1965, resulted in an attempted *coup d'état* planned to establish a national regime over the colonial one that Zhivkov was promising would go on forever. For the moment, however, all was quiet.

Little Albania, China's only ally in Europe, acted with equal consistency in the opposite direction. Radio Tirana, whose remarks are prone to exceed the limits within which the Chinese restrain themselves even more than the Bulgarian party exceeds those of the Soviets, was at no loss for an explanation:

"The policy of imperialism, propagated by the American imperialists and their lackeys, is experiencing one failure after another. This is the characteristic of our epoch which no force in the world can alter, including the modern revisionists who faithfully serve these imperialists.

"The expulsion of Nikita Khrushchev from the Presidium of the Central Committee and his release from his Government post is a heavy blow which showed the failure of his policies and the beginning of a process of decomposition in the ranks of the revisionists. At the same time, this is a great victory for Marxist-Leninists the world over, in their struggle against modern revisionism and a demonstration of the long-sighted policy of the Albanian Workers' Party."

But the Chinese themselves, whatever their shrill satellite was saying, responded to the news with surprising restraint, which boded ill for the East Europeans who had no wish for Peking and Moscow to resolve their differences. The tone of the Chinese party's message of congratulation to Brezhnev and Kosygin was strikingly different from the greetings they had sent to the Kremlin the previous May Day and on other anniversaries. These had been pointedly addressed to the "Soviet people" and not to their rulers. Now, they offered the following slogan: "The Chinese and Soviet parties and the two countries unite on the basis of Marxism-Leninism and proletarian internationalism!" There was no immediate jubilation that Khrushchev's successors were attempting to do what Peking had long proposed, to "throw him on the rubbish heap of history." That was to come later— just before they started to suggest that the same fate should befall Brezhnev and Kosygin.

10

THE OLD MAN

THE NAME OF Khrushchev had been famous in Russia for hundreds of years. Before the revolution of 1917, it belonged to one of the most ancient and aristocratic families in the tsardom, whose estates stretched along the southwestern border of the Ukraine and which, by tradition, sent its sons to serve in the imperial court. (One of them, who rose to become a distinguished Russian statesman of the late sixteenth century, was used by Pushkin as a character in his play *Boris Godunov.*) But the name had been in Nikita's peasant family for only two generations when he was born, the son of Sergei, on April 17, 1894. His grandfather had been one of the Khrushchevs' serfs, and when he was given his freedom and consequently his right to a surname, he adopted theirs. At the time of his liberation, he had been allocated a small plot of land just outside Kalinovka, one of the estate villages (which became, under Khrushchev's patronage in the 1950s, a highly favored collective settlement shown off to visiting foreign farmers) and it was here that Nikita spent the first fifteen years of his life.

It was not an auspicious start for a politician or even a revolutionary (most of whom, like Mao Tse-tung and

Fidel Castro, have middle-class origins). Khrushchev's home village of Kalinovka is situated in a remote border area in which the populations of two nations overlap and intermingle. Neither Russia nor the Ukraine, as a result, ever accepted him as one of its own, although propaganda tried to exploit each of the allegiances to which he was theoretically entitled, according to the convenience of the moment. When he was First Secretary of the Ukraine, local newspapers described him as "the finest son of the Ukrainian people," but when he assumed power in Moscow he became "the great representative of the Russian people." (It should be pointed out that the Russian word *narod*, which is usually translated as "people" for want of a more exact English equivalent, means a specific nationality—Estonian, Kazakh or Armenian, for example—and not people in general.)

Unlike Khrushchev, Stalin was always able to rely on the support of his own people, the Georgians, to such an extent that their affection and reverence for him has withstood all the exposures of his brutality and all the efforts of the authorities to purge his influence from the Soviet scene. Everywhere else in the Soviet Union, portraits of him have been destroyed, biographies of him burned and his statues smashed; but in Gori, his birthplace, the museum portraying his life and achievements has survived untouched and has recently been reopened; and when workers came to remove Stalin's monument from the middle of a square in Tbilisi, the Georgian capital, it was rumored in Moscow that six students lost their lives attempting to defend it through passive resistance in the face of Russian soldiers armed with submachine guns.

Khrushchev never learned either the Ukrainian or the

Russian language perfectly (although his Russian improved considerably over the years), but tended to speak the crude and heavily accented mixture of the two which is used in his birthplace, and which became increasingly obvious in him the more agitated he became. This explains the surprising incoherence that often overcame him when he was improvising a speech.

He once described his origins thus:

"I am a Russian of peasant stock. My grandfather was a serf, the property of a landlord who could sell him if he wished, or trade him for a hunting dog. He could neither read nor write and his life was hard. In the whole course of his life, he only had a bath twice—once when he was christened, and once when his neighbors prepared his body for burial.

"My father was a peasant farmer who worked in the mines in the winter and hoped that some day he would earn enough money to buy a horse, so that he could cultivate enough potatoes and cabbage to feed his family. He never got the horse.

"Life was no kinder to me than it had been to my parents. I was born in a farming village so poor that only one man there was rich enough to own a pair of boots. He was a peasant called "Soft Ears," and when a village boy was going to get married, he would go to Soft Ears and rent his boots to get married in. There was nothing soft about Soft Ears, apart from his name. His heart was as hard as flint: he charged the bridegroom three days' work for the hire of the boots."

Khrushchev's first school was the parish one, run by the local priest. Here, he became the first member of his family to be taught to read and write. He quickly showed that he had an outstanding memory—which he

later used to store a remarkable collection of obscure
agricultural statistics, enabling him to outargue local
agricultural administrators on their own areas' production records—by learning the Four Gospels by heart.
Impressed, the priest sent him to sit a scholarship exam-
ination at the nearest Government school in the country
town of Kursk. He failed, but for the rest of his life he
was able to draw upon his biblical knowledge (with
which he often surprised his atheist colleagues) in his
speeches and once remarked that he agreed with Christ
on many points, even if he did not accept the doctrine
of turning the other cheek. The immediate consequence
of his failure, however, was less colorful: he became the
landlord's herdsman, looking after his cattle and sheep.

Reminiscing half a century later, he used to speak bitterly about his old landlord but, paradoxically and apparently uncynically, he always maintained a show of
respect toward the landed gentry which had enslaved
his ancestors: a Canadian diplomat, descended from the
Russian aristocracy but with no ambition to be reminded of his origins, was repeatedly discomforted in
the course of negotiations in which he was involved with
Khrushchev, by the latter's insistence on addressing him
as "Count" as automatically as he would have addressed
one of his Soviet colleagues as "Comrade."

Khrushchev joined the great drift into the towns when
he was fifteen. The Russian industrial revolution was
then gathering pace, half a century later than in Western Europe, and his father, finally giving up the unequal
struggle of a peasant against weather, landlords and
hunger, took him to work in the coal pits of the Don
Basin. They went to the town of Yuzovka, a new settlement named after its Welsh founder, John Hughes, an

engineer who had opened the mine in 1869. It was owned and run by foreigners until the revolution (the best residential quarter was known colloquially as the "English compound," and the one in which Khrushchev father and son found a room, as "Dogsville"); it was here that he first came into indirect contact with the men who were to become one of his obsessional hatreds: capitalists. He recounts bitterly: "I worked at a factory owned by Germans, at pits owned by Frenchmen and at a chemical plant owned by Belgians. I discovered something about capitalists. They are all alike, whatever their nationality. All they wanted from me was the most work for the least money that would keep me alive. So I became a Communist, and all my conscious life I have worked with my whole heart and all my energy for my party."

It was not, of course, as simple as that, for it was some time before he heard of the teachings of Marx and the leadership of Lenin. In later life, he sometimes claimed that he had worked at the coal face itself ("Nowadays you miners can't imagine how intolerable conditions were: we used to work at seams less than a meter high and a meter wide"). In fact, he and his father were employed, for most of the time, as fitters in the workshops at the pit head. Relations between labor and the foreign managers were hostile, and it was on account of this that Khrushchev—according to his own account—first began to assert himself as a leader. (English engineers working in Yuzovka at the time complained that he had done so earlier than this. Innocently inviting him to join their football team, they discovered to their annoyance that "he always wanted to be center forward *and* captain.") Strikes were common, and Khrushchev soon became a member of the workers' committee that organized them, and so formed his view of capitalism by facing its stern representatives across the negotiating table.

When Russia entered World War I in 1914, he was exempted from military service as a skilled metalworker —which suggests that he was not yet politically active because the Tsar had decreed that all "undesirable elements" (a term which included then, as it does in Russia today, known opponents of the regime) be drafted automatically into the Imperial Army. As a result of his staying on in Yuzovka while his less fortunate workmates left for the front, he met for the first time the man who was later to prove his most important ally in the early stages of his climb toward political power: Lazar Kaganovich, then the local Bolshevik organizer who became Stalin's chief lieutenant in the Kremlin in the 1930s. But for some reason he has never revealed, he did not join the party for some time to come—in fact, not until 1918, a full six months after the Communists had seized power. He remained inactive during the uprisings of February and October, 1917, and finally responded to the "proletarian call to arms" in the bitter civil war against the White Guards that followed the revolution. It was while he was a junior commissar in the Red Guards that his first wife, Ksenia, a local girl whom he had married in 1916, died of starvation in the terrible famine that swept the country in the wake of war. She left behind her two children, including Khrushchev's elder son, who was later to be killed himself, as a fighter pilot in action during the battle of Stalingrad in World War II. "Life is a great school," he later recollected tranquilly. "It thrashes and bashes and teaches you."

He returned to the pit in 1920, a young widower ready to throw his life into political activity, and was immediately promoted assistant manager. (According to unconfirmed reports, he soon experienced a strike from the other side, as his angry successors on the still extant and still illegal workers' committees led protests against the unimproved conditions and the more severe food shortages.) He was also elected secretary of the local Communist cell, and thus got his foot on the first rung of the political ladder. Within two years, he had been marked by his superiors as a man to be trained for higher responsibilities. He was enrolled in one of the "workers' universities" that had been founded hastily after the revolution to provide the new class of officials, rising straight from the ranks of the proletariat, with a rudimentary higher education. He was appointed the student political organizer, and on graduation was immediately made secretary of the Petrovsko-Maryinsk district committee, controlling an area containing four small towns and eleven villages. More importantly, he was given his first taste of national politics, being elected first as a delegate to the Ukrainian Party Congress, and from there to the fourteenth All-Union Party Congress in Moscow. The latter was a tumultuous affair. Stalin had recently forced his own appointment as First Secretary, suppressing as best he could the warning against him that Lenin had dictated from his deathbed, and already displaying a brutal contempt for the principles for which the revolution had allegedly been fought and won. At this meeting, many of the delegates reacted in protest. But they were shouted down by still louder voices of the Stalinist faction in archetypal *Animal Farm* fashion. The Ukrainian delegation was reportedly one of the most strident; and one of its members

was Nikita Khrushchev. Shortly afterward, he was promoted to the party's regional headquarters in his old
home of Yuzovka, now renamed Stalino.

But here, in 1927, he experienced his first serious set-
back. Inspectors from Kiev, the Ukrainian capital, sent
down to investigate suspected malpractices, discovered
evidence of wholesale bribe-taking, drunkenness and
embezzlement among the local officials, which was so
shocking that the regional committee was completely
disbanded. There was never any suggestion that
Khrushchev himself had been actively involved in the
corruption, but he was punished at least for not having
reported it, by demotion to a minor propaganda post in
Kiev. The accused rapidly recovered—and increased—
his position by turning accuser. In his attacks on Stalin's
opposition, he not so much echoed the dictator's fury,
but anticipated its full force, employing language which
was not to become general until the show trials of the
great purges of the 1930s. He violently claimed that
"right-wingers" were guilty of "sabotaging the work of
the Central Committee," of traitorous double-dealing
within the party, and of blatant corruption. He called
for their dismissal from the party, and for their severe
punishment.

Lazar Kaganovich, who had first introduced Khrushchev to the party and had since become one of the leading members of the Ukrainian hierarchy, was transferred from Kiev to Moscow early in 1929, and in the
autumn of that year he called Khrushchev to join him
there. The party cell in the Industrial Academy, then
the nation's most prestigious school of economics, was
dominated by anti-Stalinists. Khrushchev was enrolled
as a student, charged with the task of breaking this

potentially dangerous pocket of intellectual resistance. The methods he used have never been revealed, but they were sufficiently successful for him to gain control of the cell in a matter of months, by becoming its secretary. He left the academy without attempting to take a degree, in order to become secretary of a borough party committee. In 1934, he was elected a full member of the Communist party's Central Committee, and the next year succeeded his patron, Kaganovich, who was himself promoted to the central administration, as joint secretary for the Moscow city and region. As such, he was virtually in complete control of the political, civic and economic affairs of the whole metropolis.

In spite of the war there are still today many indications of the impact his ferociously energetic leadership had on the city's growth. He mobilized every able-bodied man and woman on whom his officials could lay their hands, regardless of their normal occupation or suitability for manual labor, into Communist shock teams. Through their spare-time efforts, as they were driven relentlessly toward the fulfillment of specific construction targets, office and apartment blocks rose, and the tunnels of the infant underground railway system pushed their way toward the ever-expanding suburbs. The metro, still one of Moscow's great tourist attractions, was Khrushchev's greatest pride. Its lavish stations were planned as tributes to Stalin, with their depictions of him in mosaics, rear-lighted stained-glass windows and murals stretching from the platform to the ceiling. One of the most expensive construction projects ever undertaken in Russia at that time, it absorbed more capital investment in 1934 than the whole of light industry.

Khrushchev employed the ruthlessness with which he drove Muscovites toward providing a better city for themselves in other, more sinister, directions. Thirty years later, toward the end of his political career, thoroughly exasperated by the self-satisfied refusal of the bureaucracy to modernize its methods, he repeatedly lectured party members on the need to study and learn from managerial and technical developments in the West. But in the 1930s, his attitude was very different. (He summarized it much later in defending Russia's first baby car, the inefficient and unreliable and ill-designed Zaborozhets, against the criticisms of foreign automobile engineers: "Even excrement smells like raspberries, if it's your own.") *Evening Moscow*, a newspaper he controlled through the Moscow City Council, predicted his later opinion too early for his appreciation. It printed an article by a well-known Soviet writer, describing the economic development of Northern Italy. Khrushchev reprimanded the editorial board, stating that the progress they described was impossible in a decadent capitalist society on the verge of collapse, and that the only possible reason for publishing such an article was a desire to libel the progress of socialism. The storm died down, but the newspaper boldly repeated its offense, by printing a survey of scientific developments in the West, which it compared favorably to those in the Soviet Union. Khrushchev promptly fired the deputy editor who had been responsible, and gave a warning to the editor, which, judging by the subsequent docility of *Evening Moscow*, had its effect.

The full terror of Stalin's purges first swept through the ranks of Soviet officialdom in December, 1934. Khrushchev heralded the show trials at political rallies and in the press, calling upon the proletariat to exercise "renewed vigilance" in its search for "enemies of the people," demanding the "extermination of these vermin" and "warmly approving" the liquidations—mostly of Lenin's loyal old guard—which had already taken place. Toward the end of February, 1937, a solitary and frightened voice, which Khrushchev praised many years later for its dignified and humanitarian fury, spoke out against the persecutions at a special meeting of the Central Committee. The First Secretary of the Ukraine, Konstantin Postyshev, stood up and enumerated the rumors he had heard about mass liquidations of men who had fought heroically for the revolution. He called upon Stalin to denounce them as slanders, and to openly refute such barbarism. From the rostrum, Stalin angrily shouted at him: "Who do you think you are?"

"A Bolshevik, Comrade Stalin," he replied bitterly. "A Bolshevik." He disappeared four days later.

If Khrushchev then had any thought of exposing Stalin's depraved brutality, he effectively concealed it, and was soon rewarded for his tact. Postyshev's immediate successor in the Ukraine, Stanislav Kossior, quickly proved to be unsatisfactory as well, and he in his turn disappeared. In January, 1938, Khrushchev was sent back to Kiev by Stalin, to take over control of the party as First Secretary. At the same time, he was given his first foothold in the highest organ of the central government, the Politburo (later renamed Presidium), by being made an alternate member.

In the Ukraine itself, a reign of terror began. "Here is a warning," Khrushchev announced on his arrival in Kiev. "For every drop of the honest blood of workers that has been shed, we shall draw a bucketful of the

black blood of our enemies." It is difficult today to relate
the latter-day Khrushchev, the prosecutor of Stalinism,
the humane reformer, the suppressor of the secret police,
with the man praised in the party press, less than a year
after his take-over from Kossior, in these terms: "The
truly pitiless extermination of the enemies of the Ukrainian people began after the Central Committee sent
Comrade N. S. Khrushchev to take charge of the Ukrainian Bolsheviks." His initial threat, and this subsequent
tribute, were not empty ones: in his first five months of
power, no less than 163 of the 166 members of the
Ukrainian Central Committee had been purged, and
many of them killed. By 1940, the process had almost
repeated itself: more than one hundred of the men who
had been brought in to replace these "enemies of the
people" had themselves been liquidated. The overwhelming majority of regional organizers, and almost
the whole staff of the party's headquarters, were fired.
Some were executed, others shipped off to labor camps
in Siberia and others merely disgraced publicly. As his
campaign began to peter out, from a lack of potential
victims as much as any other cause, new territory, the
western Ukraine, came under his control through its
accession to the Soviet Union provided for in the Molotov-Ribbentrop pact. Here, he renewed his struggle
against "Ukrainian bourgeois nationalism" by deporting
thousands of his new subjects to the Eastern territories.

When the Nazis invaded Russia in 1941, and the
Politburo gave way to a State Committee for Defense
for the course of the hostilities, Khrushchev inexplicably
lost his title of alternate member. Instead, he was co-
opted on several subsidiary war councils, each of which
was responsible for one of the battlefronts. Serving as

the Kremlin's representative on these councils, with the rank of lieutenant general, he took part in planning the strategy of the Battle of Stalingrad, and of the counterattacks on the Ukrainian front.

He regained his old position in 1944, and was given the title of Prime Minister of the Ukraine, as well as that of First Secretary. The republic was in ruins, and he set about organizing its reconstruction on a pattern similar to his previous work in Moscow. But, even then, the purges went on. Tens of thousands of alleged Nazi sympathizers, who had welcomed the German troops as liberators, only to find them far more brutal than the Russian authorities, were now sent off to the labor camps, among them all the nuns and monks who could be rounded up. (Monasteries and nunneries are illegal institutions in the Ukraine to this day.) In the western Ukraine, the nationalists went underground and began to practice guerrilla warfare, which continued after open hostilities between Germany and Russia had ceased. Khrushchev's army routed them out, and—at a cost of more deportations—agricultural collectivism was enforced.

This did little to help Khrushchev to win back the favor of Moscow. In spite of his continued purges, "bourgeois nationalism" was found to be infesting the minds of the writers and academicians in his charge. The Central Committee—whose members he had selected personally—was officially reprimanded for "underestimating ideology" and many party officials were found to be lacking in a proper "sense of leadership." In 1946 there was a drought and the harvest failed. The war had eaten up and destroyed what small grain reserves there had been, and there was widespread starvation. Khrushchev was by now so unpopular with the Kremlin that he was promptly made the scapegoat. In March, 1947, he was stripped of his rank of First Secretary and allowed to keep only his more minor title of Prime Minister. Kaganovich was rushed back to Kiev by an angry Stalin in an attempt to restore control. For ten months, Khrushchev languished outside the party machine, quarreling—according to his later accounts—bitterly with his old political mentor. Kaganovich, he claimed, in one of his exposures of Stalinism, had ordered a total massacre of the "bourgeois nationalists" in the Writers' Union and the universities, but Khrushchev eventually persuaded him to moderate this to the public condemnation and imprisonment of the leading "deviationists."

Eventually, almost a year after he had arrived, Kaganovich was called back to Moscow to become a secretary of the Communist party and Khrushchev took over once more. This time, he fared better. A propaganda campaign was launched from Moscow to publicize the Ukraine's "outstanding successes" under his leadership, and late in 1949 he returned to Moscow to become the city's First Secretary again and, more important, to be elected a secretary of the Central Committee responsible for agriculture. The results were nearly catastrophic. If Stalin was responsible for the policy of enforced merger of collective farms, Khrushchev was blameworthy as well, for his brutal enthusiasm in carrying it through. In the first six months of 1950, two thirds of the collectives in the Moscow region were liquidated with the result that productivity, in the hands of the embittered peasants, sank still lower. A year later, exasperated with the defiance he had discovered, Khrushchev proposed the complete abolition of rural life. Peasants should be gathered into "agrocities," he proposed, and organized on an industrial pattern. They should be deprived of their private plots, he suggested, so that they would have no alternative but to rely on their work on the collectivized land for their livelihoods. Khrushchev's colleagues realized that the only result of this would be that the peasants would respond by ceasing to work at all—so that the previously productive private plots would soon become as barren as the nationalized land. They publicly disavowed him, and Khrushchev, in disgrace, was transferred to the party's general administration. The result of this was the opposite of what had been intended: Khrushchev once more employed all the resources of his dynamism and relentless thrust, and maneuvered himself into the position of almost sole control of the huge Communist party machine. He was careful to emphasize on every possible occasion that he was acting on Stalin's and not on his own behalf.

By March 5, 1963, the day Stalin died in his self-imposed asylum in a barricaded house outside Moscow, all the threads of the party organization were gathered neatly in Khrushchev's hands.

The story of his career since then will be familiar to readers of this book. The importance of his early career today lies in the contrast it provides with those of Brezhnev and Kosygin. Their rise through the administrative ranks was not vastly different in form, but it never involved them in Stalinist politics to any significant extent. While the West was for the most part ready to forget—or at least overlook—Khrushchev's past as one of Stalin's most prominent supporters and executives, Russians were not. When I was in Moscow, I found that survivors of his purges in the Ukraine who had moved to the capital seemed to have little difficulty in finding audiences that would listen avidly to their tales of his severity. "There was only one really important Stalinist Khrushchev never exposed," an official commented to me three months before his fall, "Khrushchev himself." The new leaders were untainted by the atrocities of the past generation of politicians, and they were the first to be so. It was a point which the public did not fail to note with some relief.

11

THE NEW MEN

IF STALIN's was the age of darkness and Khrushchev's
the age of flamboyance, Brezhnev and Kosygin's
seemed destined to become, from its first days, the age
of the faceless managers. In contrast with their predecessors, both the new First Secretary and the new Prime
Minister proved to be extremely retiring: they spent
more time working in the privacy of their offices and
less making public pronouncements from a platform or
a studio; they eschewed the lavish state receptions in
which Khrushchev had delighted; and they separated
their personal affairs from their public ones so strictly
that no outsider has yet been introduced to Kosygin's
wife. (Nina Khrushcheva, on the other hand, was made
by her husband into a world-famous personality.)
Khrushchev used to give several long interviews a year
to visiting newspaper editors from the West; neither of
the new leaders has given a single one. Khrushchev's
rambunctious enthusiasm for state visits abroad was renowned; but Kosygin commented coldly that he and his
colleagues were not in favor of "tourist trips."

Their methods of ruling are equally different, designed to suit the era of technology. Stalin basically ran

the nation's affairs from the dinner table. His ministers would gather around him in the dining room of his country house, about thirty minutes' drive from the Kremlin, and fill themselves night after night with food, vodka and brandy. When he was in a good mood, he used to organize party games before starting the business of the day, the losers of which would be "fined" by being made to drink as much as a bottle of spirits in a single draft. Then, he would sit at the head of the table and fire off a stream of orders, as they came into his head, through the early hours of the morning. In turn, the ministers would retire to the hallway outside, to relay the commands to their officials on the telephone. For those directly involved, it may have been a pleasant system of government, but for the officials it seemed otherwise, as they sat alone in their offices through the night in case they should be called. Those who were unlucky enough to be discovered to have deserted their posts to be with their families were dismissed the moment Stalin heard about it. Life was much easier under Khrushchev, and they could safely work normal office hours. But it was still perplexing, because of his habit of initiating major policy changes, apparently on the spur of the moment, in the course of a speech on a totally different topic. Some of these, as Suslov pointed out in his indictment before the Central Committee, Khrushchev never followed up. But on other occasions, he railed at officials for failing to respond to orders he had given in this capricious fashion, when they had no means of telling whether or not he intended them to be taken seriously.

Today, in the Kremlin, the rule is by committee and memorandum. If Brezhnev and Kosygin had consciously

modeled their administration on the board of directors
of a capitalist concern, they could scarcely have done
so more precisely. Their "collective leadership" has all
the deliberate impersonality of a large industrial corporation, and their avowed intention has been that it
should display a similar rationality in its decisions and
efficiency in their execution. There has been considerable speculation in the West as to how long this can
last until, as has invariably happened in Russia in the
past, a single personality rises above the rest and once
again dominates the organs of government. It is as impossible to speculate on this responsibility—some reports
have said that Brezhnev is already the dominant figure
in the partnership, others that he is on his way out—as
it is to guess whether the new dictator, if such a figure
ever emerges, would turn out to be one of the present
partners or somebody who is at present beneath them
in political rank. But there have been private assurances that the functions of First Secretary of the Communist party and Prime Minister of the state will never
again be combined in one person, and what evidence
there is suggests that all the members of the Presidium
have been taking a more equal part in the Government
since last October than they have had opportunity to do
in the past.

Neither Brezhnev nor Kosygin seems to be made of
the stuff of dictators. Kosygin, nicknamed the "Chief
Engineer" by his staff, is a technician and an administrator rather than a politician, and Brezhnev is basically an
official, rather than a revolutionary leader.

Until October, 1964, it had been difficult to imagine
two men whose fortunes were more closely tied to one
another's than Brezhnev and Khrushchev. It was Khrush-

chev who had first noticed Brezhnev as a young municipal official in a small Ukrainian town, given him his first
post in the national party administration, and taught
him the rudiments of Soviet politics; it was Khrushchev
who had arranged his successive promotions to the in-
nermost councils of the Kremlin and made it clear that
when he decided the time had come to retire, he would
like Brezhnev to succeed him; and, most ironically of all,
it was Khrushchev who had placed him in control of the
party before he went on his last, fateful holiday by the
Black Sea, and so gave him the position he needed to
overthrow his mentor.

Brezhnev is the first Communist party leader who was
too young—eleven years old, in fact—at the time of the
Bolshevik revolution to take any part in it. He had been
born in 1906, the son of a steelworker in the river port
which now bears the tortuous name of Dneprodzerzhinsk, on the banks of the Dnieper River. Today, it is
an important industrial town, with a population of two
hundred thousand, manufacturing chemicals, cement,
railway rolling stock and machine tools. At that time,
only about thirty thousand people lived there, most of
the working population being employed either in the
port or, like Brezhnev's father and later Brezhnev himself, in the iron and steel mill which had been established a few years before. He took his first job in the
mill when he was fifteen. He appeared to take little or
no interest in politics then, although Dneprodzerzhinsk
had been one of the centers of turmoil in the civil war
and, unlike many of his contemporaries, he did not join
the Young Communist League. Instead, he spent what
time he could for six years, studying at the local Technical Institute for Land Utilization and Reclamation,

and graduated as a land surveyor in 1927. Although only twenty-one, he was immediately appointed chief of a team of land utilization specialists in the Kurak provincial administration, and then promoted in rapid succession to be the deputy director of the Urals Land Administration, then director, a post which was soon coupled with the title of deputy chairman of the county's administrative committee. In 1930, he was given a scholarship to the Agricultural Institute in Moscow, where he joined the Communist party at the age of twenty-five.

He was sent back to his native town to enroll as a student in the Metallurgical Institute. The purpose of this was not primarily to train him as an engineer, but to enable him to take over the party's propaganda activities among the students, by no means all of whom had been converted to Marxist doctrine. He was graduated and returned to work as an engineer in the same steel mill as his father, but was more concerned there with the organization of propaganda and cell activities than he was with productive work. By 1937, he was head of the town's technical college and, more significantly, deputy chairman of the local executive committee (making him, in effect, deputy mayor). The following year, he became chief of the local *agitprop* (the propaganda machine) and it was as such that he was first introduced to Khrushchev.

In January, 1938, Khrushchev had been sent by Stalin to take over the control of the Ukraine as First Secretary and the purges began. As the old Bolshevik revolutionaries were swept away, Khrushchev's need for young, efficient administrators to take their places became acute. At the end of the year, Khrushchev took Brezh-

nev away from his native town, and, promoting him
through about five ranks at once, installed him as First
Secretary of the Dnepropetrovsk Regional Party Committee. As a result, at the age of thirty-two, he was governor of a thriving industrial and truck-farming region
covering more than twelve thousand square miles, including four large towns and containing a mixed population of more than two and a half million Ukrainians,
Russians, Germans and Jews (who have always been
regarded as a separate nationality in the Soviet Union)
working in iron, manganese and lignite mines, and in
smelting, chemical, engineering and food-processing
plants.

Brezhnev's career, like almost everything else in the
Soviet Union, was disrupted by the Nazi invasion in
1941—but only temporarily. Russia went to war, and
Brezhnev was commissioned a colonel in the Eighteenth
Infantry Brigade, serving in the front lines that had
been established outside Novorossisk. Khrushchev, himself a political commissar by now, had him appointed
his representative in the Eighteenth Brigade, as chief of
political administration. Again, he was put through a
series of rapid promotions and he emerged in 1943, at
the age of thirty-seven, a major general and director of
the political board of the Southern Military District. As
such, he ranked above the members of the headquarters
command, and was responsible only to Khrushchev,
who was, in his turn, answerable only to Stalin.

Some émigré organizations in the West have claimed
that his period of military rule in the south was a savage
one; but, significantly, their indictments of Brezhnev
stand out from those of other Soviet leaders of the
period, in their lack of evidence of brutality. A fairly

typical accusation published in California argues circumstantially: "Stalin's reaction to Hitler's 'betrayal' was savage—the scorched-earth policy, the detachments that mowed down [their own] Soviet troops in retreat, penalties ranging from hard labor to death for military personnel that became prisoners of the Germans even if they subsequently escaped, merciless treatment of the civilian population suspected of nonresistance or collaboration with the invaders, ruthless guerrilla operations behind the German lines. These tasks called not only for political orthodoxy, but also for resoluteness, resourcefulness, ruthlessness in a senior political officer. Had Brezhnev not demonstrated these attributes of character on the job, he would not have survived, let alone gained promotion." This may have been true, but if Brezhnev was responsible for such barbarities, it is remarkable that none of the tens of thousands of Ukrainians who fled to the West at the end of the war, full of stories of Khrushchev's atrocities, apparently knew anything about Brezhnev's involvement in them.

The war over, Brezhnev returned replete with medals to his old post in the Dnepropetrovsk region, as always under Khrushchev's supervision, and remained there until 1950. Then Khrushchev was reinstalled as First Secretary for Moscow and summoned his protégé to the capital, giving him an appointment to the headquarters of the Communist party's Central Committee. Brezhnev's function there is unknown but, true to the pattern of his career, he did not stay long. By the end of the year, he had sufficiently impressed Stalin to be appointed First Secretary to the Republic of Moldavia, which was once again a remarkable leap upward. In that capacity, he attended the last Communist party congress which Stalin held in Moscow before his death. At this nineteenth session in 1952, he declared to his subsequent embarrassment that "Comrade Stalin brilliantly combines an astonishing enthusiasm for the affairs of state with the creative development of Marxism-Leninism. Stalin is the beneficent architect of Communism. It is fortunate for our motherland that the struggle for the liberation of their nations and for the victory of Communism is led by the greatest man of our age, our wise leader and master, Josef Vissarionovich Stalin." His effusiveness was rewarded at the end of the congress, by his appointment as a candidate member of the Presidium and as one of the ten secretaries of the Central Committee.

His luck did not survive Stalin's death the next year. The "collective leadership" of Malenkov, Beria and Molotov, who took over immediate control, reduced the size of the Presidium and removed Brezhnev from the foothold he had only just gained. Khrushchev at that moment could do little to help him, but did have him transferred to the Ministry of Defense, where he became chief political commissar, a sensitive job—on account of the near rebellious state of the Soviet high command at the time—which he appears to have handled with necessary delicacy. By 1954, Khrushchev was strengthening his hold on party affairs and, in his first major defiance of Molotov, launched his Virgin Lands scheme, promising an incredulous and undernourished population not simply bread for all, but eventually free bread for all. On February 7, he sent Brezhnev to the eastern territory of Kazakhstan, where the project was to begin, as second secretary under an old-guard official, Danteleimon Ponomarenko. But the latter did not show the drive which Khrushchev sought from him, so he was transferred to Warsaw as Soviet Ambassador, and in August, 1955, Brezhnev took over full control of one of the most ambitious agricultural schemes in the history of mankind. He worked with enormous energy, scouring the whole of Russia for implements to requisition, launching labor-recruiting drives, fighting for the cooperation of officials who controlled the tractor factories and fertilizer plants; and within two years, more than two hundred million acres went under the plow for the first time.

The seed was drilled, the rain came down and the sun shone at the right times and in the required amounts; and for those first two years, the Virgin Lands confounded the soil experts and agronomists who had warned Khrushchev of the dire consequences of such a scheme, by producing bumper crops where they had said that none would grow. Brezhnev returned to Moscow in triumph for the Communist party's Twentieth Congress; Khrushchev's power was consolidating now, partly on account of the agricultural successes in the east, and he was strong enough to make his condemnation of Stalin to a closed session at the end of the meeting, and announce his program for liberalization. Brezhnev was brought back to the political center, regaining his titles of Secretary to the Central Committee and candidate member of the Presidium. His successor in Kazakhstan, Nikolai Belyayev, fared less well. In the late 1950s, the soil began to tire and the weather turned against the cultivators. Ground frost was followed by erosion, torrential rain and high winds. The yields were decimated; and Brezhnev, by now established as an expert on grain production, was sent down to investigate. Belyayev was publicly criticized and demoted for the failure.

The climax of Khrushchev's struggle for complete domination came at a meeting of the Communist party's Central Committee in June, 1957. The conflict between Khrushchev's supporters, who formed a minority in the Presidium, and the majority led by Malenkov and Molotov, came into the open, and by popular acclaim, Khrushchev won. The old party leaders, now labeled as the "antiparty group" were expelled, accused of contriving to "undermine the revolution." Brezhnev was immediately appointed to one of the vacancies in the Presidium as a full member. He began to appear as a member of delegations and reception committees with the very highest-ranking members of the new regime.

His election as President of the Soviet Union in 1960, when Khrushchev appealed to him to take over from the aging Voroshilov, who had left a session of the Supreme Soviet after an emotional outburst, made him the theoretical head of state but did little to increase his real power. His function was largely a protocol one: signing Government decrees, welcoming official delegations from abroad, accepting the credentials of new ambassadors, presiding over state receptions. But it was through his new position that Westerners were first able to come into contact with him, and view him from close quarters.

Initially, they were scarcely impressed. I first saw him at a reception in honor of a visiting crown prince from Laos. He was a stocky figure dressed in a bulky, dark brown double-breasted suit, with huge bushy eyebrows dominating his flushed face. He seemed somber and dull, and the pedestrian speech of welcome that he made to the prince reinforced this impression. While

Khrushchev and other Presidium members were surrounded by ambassadors and officials trying to make conversation with them, Brezhnev stood silent and alone, looking on.

I mentioned my disappointment at finding Brezhnev so unimposing to a Soviet official a few days later. "Don't underestimate him," he answered.

"I'm sure it's very loyal of you to say that about the head of your state," I said, "but you must agree that people with real power in this country don't become President."

"You just wait awhile," he replied. "I know your diplomats have written him off as a figurehead, but they're making a big mistake."

He was proved correct in the summer of 1963. Khrushchev was about to leave for his state visit to Yugoslavia, and was faced with the decision of deputing one of his colleagues to take charge of the affairs of state during his absence. In the recent past, this function had been carried out by Frol Koslov, whom Khrushchev had introduced to the onetime United States Ambassador to Moscow, Averell Harriman, as "my successor." But, as has already been said, Koslov had fallen out with Khrushchev a few months previously, and suffered a paralyzing stroke the previous April, which conveniently removed him from the political arena. Khrushchev selected Brezhnev and, before he left for Belgrade, reappointed him a Secretary of the Central Committee while allowing him to keep the title of President.

But even after Khrushchev's return, more and more of Brezhnev's ceremonial duties were taken over by his deputies. He no longer received ambassadors, and rarely made the journey to the airport to greet visiting delegations. He stopped making speeches almost completely. The reason for this withdrawal became apparent in July, 1964: he was finally replaced as President by Anastas Mikoyan "to allow Comrade Brezhnev to concentrate on his duties in the Secretariat." Thus he came to be in almost exactly the same position as Khrushchev had been at the time of Stalin's death; the major difference is that he did not wait for Khrushchev to die before he acted.

When he assumed power, Brezhnev maintained his facelessness in public life. In the only major speech he made in the first ten months of his reign, on agriculture, he restricted himself to his habitual, impersonal style. Behind the scenes, according to the few reports which come out of the Kremlin, he is equally unemotional and businesslike. "He is a political engineer, a pragmatist," is one semiofficial verdict. But this cold, rational exterior conceals a private joviality and penchant for wild parties, which he rarely reveals in front of strangers (although he caused a minor sensation recently, by making an elaborate display of kissing the hand of Walter Ulbricht's frostily unattractive wife Lotti when she arrived at the Moscow airport not long ago). His own wife Victoria has only once been photographed, her extremely plump figure covered in a mink coat. But his thirty-two-year-old daughter Galina, after a brief career as a film starlet, is now a well-known journalist; his eldest son works in the Ministry of Foreign Trade and was recently a member of a delegation that visited Britain, when Soviet Embassy officials in London repeatedly refused to state whether he was even related to the current First Secretary; and his youngest, twenty-year-old Mikhail, is a student at the Faculty of Journalism at

Moscow University and has a part-time job on *Izvestia* (a fact that officials have also tried to keep secret). Brezhnev himself has the unusual distinction for a politician of being known as a collector of antique timepieces and a keen amateur ornithologist, with one of the best collections of stuffed birds in Moscow.

If little is known about Brezhnev as a man, still less is known about the even more retiring Alexei Kosygin. Their very lack of public personality appears to be a deliberate contribution to the roles they have assigned themselves, as reasoned, skilled professionals rather than the prima donna they succeeded.

        *   *   *   *   *

In 1944, General de Gaulle went to Moscow and was received by Stalin in his Kremlin office. During the course of their conversation, de Gaulle suddenly asked him: "How do you prepare your famous plan?"

"I do nothing," Stalin replied, turning to a palefaced, bespectacled young man by his side. "He does it. He is the plan."

Fourteen years later, Khrushchev went to Paris, and was questioned by a group of industrialists there on various technical points of Soviet economic development. Khrushchev turned to the same man Stalin had praised, and said: "Address yourself to Kosygin. He takes precedence over me in these matters."

Alexei Kosygin was born in 1904, two years before Brezhnev and two weeks after Russia went to war with Japan. Lenin had resigned from the Social-Democrat Labor Party and was losing ground to the opposition within the socialist movement itself. The year before, he had achieved a narrow victory at the Second Communist

Party Congress largely because the delegations that had intended to vote against him had walked out in protest before they had had an opportunity to do so. He was now thinking of abandoning politics and emigrating to the United States. Stalin had just escaped from his first term of imprisonment in a Siberian Labor camp, and hidden himself in a peasant cottage in the heart of the Caucasus, where, in due course, he fell in love with and married his protector's daughter, Catherine Svanidze. Khrushchev was ten, and working as a cowherd in his native village of Kalinovka. "Bloody Sunday," when first signs of revolution among Russian workers were to be suppressed by the Imperial Guard, was a year away.

Kosygin was born in one of the poorest quarters of St. Petersburg, the son of a lathe operator. Beyond this, nothing is known of his early years; but, unlike Khrushchev and Brezhnev, he was a Communist from the very beginning of his maturity, joining the Red Army at the age of fifteen, in 1919, when its victory over the White Guard was still far from certain. At the end of the civil war, he was demobilized to register as a student in the Technical College of what was now Petrograd, to take a training course in the organization of producer and consumer co-operatives. In 1924, he was assigned to Siberia. The situation there was unfavorable to the Bolsheviks, because the co-operatives, which had grown to be a considerable political as well as economic force, were still in the control of Social Democrats and other non-Communists. The function of twenty-year-old Kosygin and his young colleagues was to penetrate the co-operative movement, and reorganize it as an adjunct of the party. He worked as an instructor in co-operation in the Irkutsk area, and then became manager of the planning

department of the Siberian Territorial Union of Co-
operatives. While he was there, he became a member of
the Young Communist League and, in 1929, was sent
back to Leningrad to enroll in the Textile Institute,
where he spent six years studying to become an engineer. This set the pattern of his career. After an early
start in politics, he abandoned the party ladder up which
Khrushchev was then climbing, with Brezhnev following behind, and became an industrial administrator
instead. He was rapidly promoted from foreman to
departmental manager in one plant, and was then appointed director of the large October Textile Factory
in Leningrad in 1937. Here, he attracted the attention
of Andrei Zhdanov, a stern ideologist whom Stalin had
placed at the head of the revolutionary city. Zhdanov
promoted him to manager of the huge industrial
transport department, which was responsible for all
freight activities in the Leningrad region. By October,
1938—three months after his previous promotion, and
at the age of thirty-four—he was elected chairman of
the Leningrad City Soviet of Workers' Deputies, or in
other words, mayor. The next year, Zhdanov was called
to Moscow by Stalin, to become a leading member of
the Communist party Secretariat, and he brought Kosygin with him to the capital, to become people's commissar (minister) for the textile industry—a post which he
took up only four years after his graduation as a student
from the Textile Institute. It was a tough job, newly created in response to the public outcry against the severe
shortages of clothing and textiles then prevailing.
Within two months of assuming this post, he was made
a member of the Central Committee and appointed to
the sixty-two-member commission led by Stalin to revise

the third five-year plan, after considering the requests flooding in from people working in the various sectors of the economy. In a conventional speech to his colleagues, he said that Soviet progress had "shown up the capitalist nations in all their rottenness" and attempted to demonstrate, through statistics, that the textile industries of England, the United States, Japan and France were "marching backward." But his honesty, for a Russian official working under Stalin, was nonetheless remarkable: even if the Soviet textile industry expanded at the rate proposed in the plan, he stated, it would still lag behind those of the four countries he had mentioned. He described a sixteen-point program he had drawn up to supplement the plan, in an attempt to "meet the people's rightful demands."

One year and five months later, before he had had opportunity to do more than lay the foundations for his planned expansion of the textile industry, Kosygin was promoted again, this time to a place in the Council of Ministers itself. He was also made a member of the Economic Council, where he gradually took control of forward planning for the whole of Soviet industry. At the outbreak of war, he joined Mikoyan on the Council for Evacuation and began to organize the complex machinery that had been hurriedly set up to move a large part of the civilian population of urban Russia to safety in the eastern territories. He returned to his native city, and organized the evacuation of half a million Leningrad citizens, winning the official commendation that he "gave to the evacuation a sense of priority which it had lacked until then, and improved the efficiency of transportation." He moved to the east with the évacués to create from almost nothing a munitions industry safely away from the front lines. Years later, the official *Soviet History of the Great Patriotic War* (a title which the Russian authorities insist on giving to World War II) said that "the defense industry's productive capacity had to be increased in a period of between eighteen months and two years by two and a half times its previous level, by means of constructing new factories, mostly in the east, and transferring other branches of industry to arms manufacture. The great organizational work that achieved this exceptionally complex and difficult task was carried out by leading party and Government officials," who, it said, included Stalin, Khrushchev, Mikoyan and Kosygin. By 1943, Kosygin was the Prime Minister of the Russian Federation, responsible for more than two thirds of the territory of the Soviet Union, still containing in spite of the evacuations more than half the population. Despite the nation's desperate position at that stage of the war, Kosygin was already turning his attention to public welfare, a field which his colleagues under Stalin had sadly neglected. He told the Supreme Soviet in January, 1944, that he intended to introduce compulsory education for children aged seven and over; young people whose schooling had been disrupted by the war would be given free tuition in their spare time; the amount of accommodation in children's homes within the Federation was to be doubled, to accommodate the 1,100,000 children who had been orphaned in the hostilities. (Significantly, Kosygin's was the only state in the Soviet Union that ever revealed the extent of this human tragedy.)

Turning to economic affairs, he stressed the need for supplies to be rushed to the civilian populations of areas liberated from the Germans. Production of furniture,

cutlery, glassware and crockery had been satisfactorily
increased to meet these demands, he said, but there had
been too many shortcomings in other fields. The shortage of footwear was particularly dire, he said, and he
criticized the shoe industry for carrying out 30 per cent
fewer repairs than it had done in 1940. Even then, his
attitude was outstandingly un-Stalinist. His speeches
lacked the grandiloquence of his political contemporaries and they were sometimes humdrum in content.
But they demonstrated a concern for public well-being
and a down-to-earth attitude that the others, in their
patriotic fervor and almost religious obeisance to Stalin,
lacked.

It was probably his refusal to involve himself in politics, rather than administration, which enabled him to
survive the new outbreak of purges in the late 1940s.
His sponsor, Zhdanov, had died of a heart attack in the
autumn of 1948, and the purge of Leningrad officials
whom Stalin had insanely accused of plotting to dis-
member Russia began soon afterward. Nikolai Voznesensky, one of Kosygin's colleagues in the Council of
Ministers, and Alexander Kuznetsov, a leading party
official, were liquidated; but Kosygin himself survived,
apparently on the intervention of Mikoyan and Malenkov, who argued with Stalin that he was completely
loyal, in spite of the fact that he had come from Leningrad. But, interestingly, a Russian defector who was in
Leningrad at the time, and was in close contact with
Kosygin during his visits to the city, reports that Kosygin became drunk at a birthday party he attended late
one night and referred to Stalin as a "pockmarked bas-
tard," adding words to the effect that the Soviet Union
could become a great country, and the achievements of

socialism could be consolidated, if only the dictator could be removed. There is little reason to doubt this story, because it is in the interests of most defectors to denigrate the political leaders of the country they have left, not to praise their lack of involvement in the terrors of the past.

The remark could not have been made in the presence of a secret police informer, for at this time Kosygin was put in temporary charge of the Ministry of Finance, in order to investigate and stamp out the massive inefficiency, fraud, falsification of records, and embezzlements of which hundreds of its officials were found to be guilty. After this cleaning-up operation, he was transferred back to light industry and textiles, a sector of the economy that had been almost completely destroyed in the war, and then neglected by the planners responsible for its postwar reconstruction.

Then, for a time, his fortunes fell. Some reports say that he was saved from liquidation only because Stalin died before he could order it. He was dismissed from the Council of Ministers for no apparent reason—although at the same time he was put in charge of food distribution, which had been woefully inefficient. But the new plan, announced in September, 1953, called for a "sharp rise" in living standards, and it was clear that Kosygin was the only man in the Government capable of achieving it. His ministry was renamed as that of Industrial Consumer Goods and, in December, he was reappointed to the Council of Ministers with over-all responsibility for the drive to improve the material conditions of the Russian people. He made a major speech on this subject at the Twentieth Congress of the party, which was, once again, remarkable for its lack of political content. He described the problems with which he was faced in this project, and stressed the need to co-ordinate short-term objectives with long-range plans. Because this had not been done in the past, he claimed, the economy had been gravely unbalanced. The whole system of planning should be reformed, he said, and as a start, the draft five-year plan before the congress should be scrapped. His boldness resulted in his appointment as first deputy chairman of the State Planning Board, and he gave up his place in the Council of Ministers once again, to concentrate exclusively on carrying out the reforms he had proposed.

With the rise of Khrushchev, Kosygin's powers rapidly increased. Khrushchev made him First Deputy Prime Minister in March, 1958. At the Twenty-first Congress a year later, he again sharply criticized planning methods. This time, Khrushchev responded by making him chairman of the State Planning Board and a full member of the party Presidium. Then, at the Twenty-second Congress, he made the first major political pronouncement of his career. It was controversial, in that it went much further in condemning Stalinism and Stalinists than any of his colleagues' speeches. "We must and shall do all we can to purge the cult of personality from our party and our society, to cut off its shoots and dig up its roots." He attacked Molotov and his associates for interfering in economic affairs to the extent that they "created conditions in which it was impossible to work."

It was with these attitudes, and from his position as Khrushchev's immediate deputy in the Council of Ministers, that he assumed power with Brezhnev in October, 1964. He became the first Soviet Prime Minister to have risen through the ranks of industrial administration and the organs of state, rather than the party. The most significant thing about his career was that he had never held a post in the Communist party, except in connection with the posts he had held in the Government. It was a sign of remarkable progress in the Soviet Union that its Government was finally in the hands of a man whose first loyalty was to the Government and not to the party.

Since he came to power, Westerners who have met him in Moscow have mostly expressed respect for his "no-nonsense" efficiency. But perhaps the most remarkable tribute which he received has come from one of the most unlikely sources imaginable—a leading figure in the anti-Communist movement organized among Soviet Russian émigrés in the West, Sergei Kungurtsev, who worked with Kosygin in the textile industry before the war: "He was a considerate boss, with a complete mastery of business methods. He treated his assistants extremely well, stood up for them when they spoke for business interests against political expediency. Even at the height of the political purges of saboteurs in the late 1930s, he did not succumb to the prevailing hysteria, but maintained his rationality and calm."

12

THE NEW MOOD
IN RUSSIA

BEHIND THE scenes in Russia, Brezhnev and Kosygin worked quickly to establish the new regime's less flamboyant, more coldly businesslike character, in the people they chose to represent it. Khrushchev's personal protégés disappeared from their seats around the throne, to be replaced by less well-known professionals from the "apparatus" who shy away almost instinctively from anything suggestive of personal publicity. Alexei Adzhubei lost the editorship of *Izvestia* at the same time as his father-in-law was removed from the leadership of the country, and was then expelled from membership in the Central Committee in November, protesting—according to one man who was present—that he had never really supported Khrushchev in the first place, and was now entirely ready to serve the new regime in his old capacity. Instead, he was made fiction editor of a monthly picture magazine, *Soviet Union,* produced by the Foreign Languages Publishing House primarily for distribution abroad; and, according to his colleagues, he appears resigned to his fate. At *Izvestia,* he was replaced by a long-serving ideological official, Vladimir Stepakov, subsequently appointed head of the powerful Propaganda and Agitation Department of the Central Committee. The others fell soon afterward: Vladimir Lebedev, Khrushchev's powerful private secretary who had run his private office and his independent research organization and, it is believed, had written many of his more colorful speeches; Oleg Tryankovsky, the suave, American-educated son of a former Russian Ambassador to Washington, who had been Khrushchev's personal adviser on foreign affairs, and who had maintained direct lines of communication with a few carefully chosen United States officials; and Alexander Shuysky, Khrushchev's expert on agricultural policy, who presumably shared some of the blame for his employer's catastrophic failures in that field. Nothing has been heard of any of them since, but this fact should not be taken to have the sinister innuendo it would have had under Stalin or even Khrushchev. There is no reason to doubt that they are still alive and that they have not been exiled, but given humble posts in Moscow instead, in exchange for maintaining silence.

Adzhubei's colleagues in Khrushchev's much-suspected "press group," whom Suslov had reprimanded before the Central Committee for acting as their master's and not the party or the state's voice, also went with him into obscurity. Mikhail Kharlamov, the chairman of the State Committee for Radio and Television, was particularly humiliated by receiving his dismissal—although he publicly denied knowledge of it at the time—while he was still in Oslo, as the guest of the Norwegian State Broadcasting Corporation. Kharlamov had been exceptionally well known in the West as an "amiable Russian"; he had been a leading figure in the diplomatic community in Washington when he had edited *USSR* magazine as a counselor in the Soviet Embassy there, and had become a card-playing acquaintance of President Kennedy's press secretary, Pierre Salinger. Now, he was made a text editor in the State Publishing House for Political Literature. Victor Satyukov, the rather austere, gray-haired father figure of Moscow journalism, who was editor of *Pravda*, survived slightly longer. When he returned from Paris, where he had been leading a Soviet parliamentary delegation at the time of Khrushchev's fall, he apparently persuaded the new leaders that he had always maintained a greater independence of Khrushchev than the other members of the press establishment, and won a reprieve. By October 19, he was feeling sufficiently secure to publicly denounce Western correspondents he met at a Kremlin reception as "cold-war provocationists" for reporting rumors that he had already been fired. But less than a month later, on November 12, they came true: he threw away the second chance he had been given, by publishing an editorial condemning proposals for economic reform although it was by then obvious to almost everyone—even to foreigners—that Kosygin supported them and intended to put them into practice. He was removed and within three days, after a successor had been appointed, *Pravda*'s economic policy was reversed by editorials pleading the opposite case to Satyukov's.

More than in any other change, however, the mood of the new regime was symbolized by the fall of one man and the rise of another, neither of whose professions seems, at first sight, to be closely linked with the world of politics. The man who fell—the Ukrainian geneticist Trofim Lysenko—already had an established reputation as one of the great charlatans of the modern age. His scientific claims were as preposterous as those of the medieval alchemists, but they were far more dangerous because they promised the transformation of living things, not of mere metals. He first emerged into public life from an agricultural research center in the Ukraine in the mid-1930s, when he bombarded newspapers and party organizations with a paper he had written suggesting that existing strains of spring wheat could be given potential yields as high as those of rye, simply by subjecting the seeds to a simple form of temperature treatment. This ostensibly effected the change by simulating the climatic conditions in which rye flourishes. Although experiments quickly proved that this was untrue, Lysenko had by that time been turned into a national figure by the enthusiastic publicity and official praise he had received for his "solution" to Russia's bread shortage, and he went on undeterred by the derision of his scientific contemporaries to make ever more grandiose claims on the basis of his already discredited theory. Soon, he was publicly propounding his almost universally ridiculed theory, to the applause of party devotees up and down the country. This was that characteristics acquired by one generation in response to environment are passed on to the next by inheritance. Its personal fascination for Stalin, to whom Lysenko found he had ready access, was disturbingly clear. If this theory could be exploited in plants and animals through creating artificial environments, it could also be applied to human beings. Thus, to put it into its crudest terms, it meant that, in the socialist environment of the Soviet Union, undesirable "bourgeois" characteristics could eventually be bred out of the population and the new generation, heralded by Young Communist League propaganda, of men and women who were purely Communist by nature would not be subject to the vagaries of persuasion or capable of the sins of compromise or deviation. This aspect of Lysenkoism was never emphasized in public, perhaps because of the unsavory similarity it bore to the Nazi theory of the superrace, and the realization that, to be fully effective, it would involve the mating of only carefully selected human couples. Lysenko pointed out in another context that ideal conditions would eventually produce cows with unusually high milk yields, but to perpetuate this trait, it would be essential to mate only the progeny of animals that possessed it. Crossbreeding, he believed, would dilute the characteristic, not disseminate it.

By 1948, Lysenko's theory had achieved the status of an article of Stalinist faith, and consequently was no longer challengeable on rational or scientific grounds. His critics made a last attempt to expose him at a turbulent meeting of the All-Union Academy of Agricultural Sciences that year, until one of them ended all discussion by asking Lysenko what was now the only relevant question: "What does the Central Committee (a constitutional euphemism for Stalin) think of your ideas?"

"The Central Committee is acquainted with my views and thoroughly approves of them," Lysenko replied with devastating finality. He had earlier driven home this point to his doubting colleagues, by arranging for one of the most prominent among them, Professor Nikolai Vavilov, to be transported to a Siberian labor camp, where he died in captivity.

Hopes for the re-establishment of scientific standards in Russian genetics rose on Stalin's death. In April, 1956, Lysenko was forced to resign as director of the Institute of Genetics and Khrushchev arranged for Professor Vavilov to be posthumously "rehabilitated." But Lysenko was not in the cold for long; the fascination of a science which could change the nature of man in a Communist society came to grip Khrushchev as effectively as it had done his predecessor. In 1958, with his new patron's public blessing, Lysenko returned to prominence. He regained control of the official journal of genetics, and dismissed those of his critics—who had only recently regained their posts—who had not already resigned in fruitless protest. Three years later, he was reinstated as director of the Institute of Genetics and his grip over the Soviet study of this field was once more complete. Papers attacking him were privately circulated among students and officials; Khrushchev's then minister of agriculture, Mikhail Olshansky, called these accusations "monstrous."

Within ten days of Brezhnev and Kosygin's taking over the Kremlin, however, Lysenko's power began to crumble. The press, inspired by a confidential directive from above, launched a series of attacks on him and the despotic methods he had used to impose his farcical theory on a supposedly rational society. The first appeared on October 23, in the Young Communist League's mass circulation newspaper, *Komsomolskaya Pravda*. Appropriately, it had been written by Vladimir Dudintsev, whose novel, *Not by Bread Alone*, which had pleaded for the liberalization of ideas in Russian scientific and technological thought, had been severely criticized in the Soviet Union in 1956, and who had been disgraced when it appeared, against the wishes of the authorities, in translation in the West. Since then, he had been privately chronicling Lysenko's misdeeds and the persecution of his critics such as Professor Vavilov, in the hope that the moment would eventually arrive when it might be possible to expose him. With the fall of Khrushchev, that moment had come, and in his article, Dudintsev accused Lysenko of "exterminating the flower of Soviet biology," by introducing the Stalinist practice of denunciation into scholarly debate. Those opponents of Lysenko who had not been removed from their posts, he said, had in many cases been broken by him, and had spent their most active years as researchers engaged on work which they knew to be useless at best, and for the most part destructive.

Then, it was revealed that Lysenko had for years been falsifying the crop and cattle-breeding statistics of his experimental farm at Gorki, in order to conceal his failures. A writer who made a tour of inspection of the farm reported sarcastically to *Literaturnaya Gazeta:* "I do not share the extreme views of some scientists, who maintain that Lysenko's experiments failed to produce anything that was either novel or valid. A lot of things one can see at Gorki are novel, and a lot of them are valid. But, as a wise man once remarked in another context, what is novel is invalid, and what is valid is not novel." After some weeks of silence, one of the members of the Reuters bureau in Moscow telephoned the Institute of Genetics and asked for the name of the director. "It's not Lysenko any more," he was told. A few days later, it was announced in the press that Lysenko's chief scientific lieutenant, Mikhail Olshansky, had been relieved of the chairmanship of the Academy of Agricultural Sciences. Olshansky's successor was Pavel Lobanov, who had been chairman during the period of Lysenko's first disgrace, but who had been overthrown by him after his return to favor, in 1961. It is significant that, although Lobanov has scientific qualifications, he is primarily a politician and has been a deputy prime minister and a deputy chairman of the State Planning Committee. His reappointment implies not merely that he has returned to official favor after years of obscurity, but that the new leaders wanted a strong, official arm in the academy to sweep away Lysenkoism as well as Lysenko himself, and to ensure that Soviet geneticists would have sufficient official backing to restore their respectability in the scientific world. It marked the end of a long, sad period for an important area of Soviet thought where Stalinism had continued, under Khrushchev's approving eye, long after Stalin's influence had been swept away elsewhere.

As the era of Stalin and Khrushchev was brought to its end in genetics, the new age of the Kremlin technocrats began to show itself more positively in the all-important sphere of economics. While Lysenko was falling to his disgrace, another Ukrainian, Yevsei Liberman, an economist who has become almost as famous in a much shorter time and for more honorable reasons, was rising rapidly to the head of the new movement for industrial reform. It had begun to make tentative progress in Khrushchev's last years, but had quickly bogged down in the quagmire of the Communist planners. A professor of economics at Kharkov University, Liberman was educated in the tradition of Russian liberal thought at a private gymnasium (secondary school) and the Faculty of Law at Kiev University before the revolution; and it is that undogmatic attitude in his scholarly background that he is expressing today in his statements on contemporary Russian problems, with the approval of his new sponsors, Brezhnev and Kosygin. In the midst of the tangled controversy between various factions of Marxist-Leninist economists, his ideas—although they have been seriously misinterpreted in the West—emerge with refreshing directness and simplicity. The Soviet economy, he says, has grown to be too huge and diversified to be controlled centrally any longer, and the efficiency of individual factories and of whole industries should be measured in the future by the profits they produce on the capital invested in them, instead of their ability to fulfill some theoretical plan worked out by a bureaucrat isolated from reality by the confines of his office. Because the fulfillment of these plans had become an end in itself, many concerns thrived by producing unusable goods, simply because they produced enough of them to achieve the targets officially laid down. Under Liberman's system, such organizations would go bankrupt and the capital they would otherwise have squandered through repeated losses could be gainfully employed in expanding other sectors of the economy that show evidence of fulfilling a need rather than a plan. In Britain and in the United States, many newspaper editorial writers have applauded this view with more optimism than accuracy, as an indication that Russia is at last admitting to the failure of its Communist planning, and returning to a modified form of capitalism. The truth is otherwise, as Liberman himself points out: he is in no way challenging the state's right to its monopoly of capital, but rather trying to increase it more rapidly than has been the case in the past, by giving it a greater flexibility to respond to economic stimuli.

For fifteen years after the revolution, Liberman was himself a planner, and formulated his new system from his bitter experiences of the prevailing one. He worked in a total of four plants, including a six-year stint as chief planning officer in a factory making agricultural machinery of questionable quality, which was sold by the simple expedient of having the authorities order collective farm managements to buy them. During the war, he was transferred to a Government post in Moscow, and in 1945 he went to Kharkov as a teacher in the Institute of Engineering and a part-time consultant to local factories. Studying in his spare time, he earned his doctorate in 1956, at the age of fifty-seven, and was given his professorship three years later.

It was also in 1956 that he first presented his views, as an unknown provincial academician, to the limited audience provided by the party's monthly theoretical journal *Communist*. Unnoticed by the general public, and passed over by Western commentators as the minor heresy of an insignificant Ukrainian theorist, his article struck a responsive chord in the minds of other and better-known Russian economists with progressive ideas, who had been too timid themselves to air them publicly. Among them were two men of national standing: Vasily Nemchinov, the distinguished statistician who died within a few days of Khrushchev's fall, just too soon to witness the breakthrough from the age of centralized planning; and Valery Trapeznikov, the Academy of Science's leading expert on automation. Liberman soon became their spokesman.

Their first major opportunity came just before the Communist party's Central Committee met to discuss the growing urgency for industrial reform at the end of 1962. *Pravda* gave Liberman space to put the progressives' case to the delegates before they assembled, and to the astonishment of its more informed readers, he did so. The more emphasis the state placed on profits, he stated, the greater the incentive would be for factories to improve the quality of their goods and increase the efficiency of their production. The reaction of the Soviet economic establishment was summed up by the indignant question of one Leningrad planner: "What does he want? Industrial anarchy?" Nemchinov, by now blind and reaching the end of his life, came out of retirement to suggest that planning decrees should be scrapped in favor of a system of tenders, in which the Government advertised the orders it wished to place with various industries and accepted the lowest bid offered. Trapeznikov entered the discussion as well, to deny that there was anything "capitalistic" about the idea that capital should be made to earn interest.

But by the time the discussion reached the floor of the Central Committee in November, the conservatives had been alerted. "Lenin put forward the principle of organization against *laissez faire* and petit bourgeois negligence, against opportunism and anarchy," said one, and another: "We must never forget that the unique centralization of planning is one of the great victories of the socialist regime. We must not weaken, but improve planning." And a third: "If we give up the centralized planning of salaries, production, costing and investment, we give up the state's regulation of the most important parts of the economy—in fact, of economic planning. This path is fraught with danger."

In the Central Committee, which was chaired by Khrushchev, their rear-guard action won them a definite, if temporary, victory. The progressives' proposals were to be put to the test, it was decided, but on such a minute scale—in one factory tailoring men's suits and in a second making women's dresses—that the results of the experiment would be far too narrow to justify anybody's drawing any general conclusions from them. At the same time, Khrushchev's rival proposal for industrial reform was accepted, which had the advantage to many of those present at the meeting of increasing rather than diminishing bureaucratic control over the economy. In essence, industry was to be taken out of the hands of the governmental ministries, and become the direct and exclusive responsibility of the Communist party and its "apparatus." To facilitate this—and, as has been pointed out previously, to reorganize agricultural administration at the same time—the party was to be divided into two distinct branches, one for industry and one for agriculture.

In the resulting confusion, Liberman and his fellow progressives were forced to retreat from the limelight to the specialized economic and theoretical journals; meanwhile, the rest of the nation faced a proliferation of new committees which Khrushchev's move had brought into existence, it turned out, to supplement rather than to replace the old ones. The stories of economic chaos in Russia were already too familiar and too numerous to bear repetition, but they became still worse. To give only one example, the director of a large engineering plant in Leningrad discovered that he was now responsible to no less than twenty separate committees, and that if he succeeded in persuading one of them to give him its authority to make some change, another would surely deny it to him, taking several months to decide to do so. His design department had created a new version of a machine tool which would have cost only fractionally more to produce than the current model, but which would have been—in the director's opinion—so superior to any of its rivals that it would result in considerable economies for its purchasers. Some committees agreed with his claim, but others rejected it purely on the basis that the new design would cost more than the old; so it never went into production.

He had wanted to hire one particularly brilliant engineer to replace three existing ones, but could not do so because he could not get the permission he needed to pay him more than each of the three had been earning individually, on the grounds that it would be "uneconomic" to do so. He had wanted to stop production for a short period in one of his workshops, so that structural repairs could be carried out; but the committees insisted that arrangements should be made for production to continue at the same time as the repair work, although this course would be far more expensive than the alternative of paying production workers overtime later to make up for the time lost.

Quietly, the experiment went under way in the course of 1963. The Mayak (Lighthouse) men's tailoring plant and the Bolshevichka (Woman Bolshevik) fashion house had their plans canceled, and were given the unprecedented right to negotiate sales directly with retail stores. At first, they had difficulty in obtaining supplies from suspicious textile plants, but the buying departments of the stores themselves were delighted. The two plants guaranteed to supply them only what they ordered—designs were discussed at length between the two parties, which had not been the case before—and made their deliveries on time.

Quality improved radically, because workers were

paid piece-rate bonuses only for producing goods that were salable, not those which merely served to swell production figures in a distant planning office. Bolshevichka established a market research department. Mayak reformed its production lines and considerably reduced the amount of labor needed for each job. Turnover shot up; profits increased by 7 per cent; the prices of the clothes they manufactured dropped, on an average, 12 per cent; and the wages of the workers went up by about 15 per cent.

But until Khrushchev went, nothing more was done. A few press reports commented on the success of the experiment, and one or two bolder editors suggested that it should now be extended. Then, Alexei Kosygin came to power and called for "the establishment of economically justified prices; an increased role for profits; and an obligatory and systematic scheme of material incentives for good productive labor." These, he said, "are preconditions if our economy is to grow more rapidly."

The conservatives did not give up, but found new hope for centralized planning in electronic computers. Academician Federenko described, in January, 1965, his dream of a nationwide computer chain which would control the whole economy. Liberman replied: "Some economists seem to believe that the introduction of a large number of electronic computers could radically improve planning, even if one leaves its present methods untouched." One of his allies, Ivan Malyshev, the deputy director of the Central Statistics Board, was more direct: "Do you expect to be able to see from the main computing center all our vast territory from the rocks of Murmansk to the flaming sunshine of Kolkhida, to see how people sow and reap, how every chemical complex functions, how every machine works? If something goes wrong in Khabarovsk, can you merely press a button in Moscow and correct it? What a strange Utopia! Society is not the sum of mathematical zeros and digits. It is a living, creative body."

But such outcries were by now unnecessary. Liberman and his colleagues had almost won the day.

Two weeks after Khrushchev's fall, the National Economic Council, the body responsible for the over-all direction of Soviet industry, pronounced its long-awaited verdict on the experiments in the two clothing factories. They had been outstandingly successful, it said, and published a draft decree placing one third of the whole clothing and shoemaking industries under the new, profit-conscious system. Kosygin welcomed this at a session of the Supreme Soviet a month later, and announced that its scope would soon be broadened considerably. "We will start planning on the basis of customers' demands, not only in the consumer goods industries, but in other branches of the economy as well," he promised the delegates. In December, he ordered that heavy industrial enterprises in the Lvov area of the Ukraine, including foundries, engineering works and a coal mine should be included in the scheme, and in January, 1965, the National Economic Council approved a further list of four hundred factories manufacturing consumer goods, which were to follow on April 1. Within two months, the coal mine was reported to have increased productivity to well above the targets set for it, reducing labor costs at the same time.

By March, Kosygin was lecturing the planners on the shortcomings of their methods: "In the past, recommendations from above were often based on subjective considerations and were in contradiction to the economic laws of socialism. The approach was, in fact, economically illiterate, and it was reflected in national economic plans and in memoranda and in the press. Many of its false conclusions are still taken by many local officials to be guideposts for planning.

"In considering important questions, we are often the prisoners of dogmas of our own creation, and it is high time to replace them with a new set of principles that apply to modern industrial conditions. Today, as well as in the past, many mistakes are made in planning, which often appear to be a result of a bureaucratic approach.

"We must free ourselves. We must free ourselves from everything that has bound the planners, and somehow forced them to prepare their plans in a way which conflicts with the needs of the nation's economy. We must ensure a more rapid rate of improvement in living standards. Wages must be placed in a direct relationship with increases in productivity."

Brezhnev followed Kosygin's lead by calling for the application of progressive ideas to agricultural problems as well. He told officials to purge their minds of old dogmas and to apply themselves to finding means of putting collective and state farms on a profitable basis. As a start, he announced the cancellation of all collective farms' past debts to the state, which totaled two billion rubles (about $224 million), and ordered an immediate increase in the prices they were offered for deliveries of produce to the state. The quotas for such supplies were to be drastically pruned, he said, so that they would relate in the future to the farms' actual potential, not to the optimistic and unrealistic demands of planning officers. He instructed the party to work out a new wage structure for farm workers, which would enable them to earn large incentive bonuses. Previously, he said, the planners had forced farms to grow crops which the farmers themselves knew to be unsuitable for the land on which they were cultivated. In the future, he directed, the chairman of collective and state farms must be "free in fact, not just in words" to assert the independence promised them in a decree ten years ago but never actually honored. They were to decide for themselves which crops to cultivate and by what methods, without interference from party officials.

But his most radical move was to reverse Khrushchev's campaign against what he had called the "unsocialist instinct for private ownership." In the early 1960s, Khrushchev had ordered a series of restrictions to be imposed on peasants who cultivated private plots in their spare time, and who, because of the inadequacies of the state retail system, were able to sell their produce in urban markets for far higher prices than those charged in state-controlled shops. His intention had been to remove the incentive to spend time on one's private plot, instead of on the collective land; and in the course of the next three years, the amount of land privately cultivated fell by 20 per cent; peasants owning more than one cow and a calf, two pigs and a goat were ordered to sell the surplus livestock, and almost penal taxes were imposed on them, based on official estimates of the value of their produce. The result, as Brezhnev and many others realized, was merely to reduce the amount of food available from private plots, without in any way increasing the productivity of state and collec-

tive farms. Indeed, the peasants were so disgruntled
that many of them devoted still less effort to their collective tasks than they had before. Khrushchev's limita-
tions were "unfounded," Brezhnev told the planners. "It
is wrong to disregard the potentialities of private plots
cultivated by collective farmers, industrial workers and
office employees to satisfy their personal requirements.
Unwarranted restrictions have been imposed in this
sphere in recent years, despite the fact that economic
conditions were not ripe for such a step." Private plots
had occupied 3 per cent of cultivated land in the Soviet
Union, he revealed, and produced about one third of
the nation's food.

Kosygin turned his attention to one of the most urgent
problems in the Russian struggle to improve living
standards: housing. Here again, the new leaders reversed Khrushchev's determined campaign to abolish
private ownership. Instead of the old boasts of municipal and co-operative housing for all, in huge blocks of
apartment buildings, Kosygin frankly admitted that "the
housing problem is still far from being solved" with an
honesty that his audience must have found refreshing.
As in agriculture, Khrushchev's restrictions on housing
construction had served mostly to create a new shortage.
In 1962, he had decreed that "houses are to be confis-
cated, without compensation, from citizens who have
paid for their erection out of unearned income." Ostensibly, this was a measure to stop racketeers from spending
their illegal profits; but because one had to prove if
challenged in a court of law not only that every kopek
one had paid for the house had been earned through
honest labor, but also that all the materials used in its
construction had been legally acquired, it militated

against the majority of comparatively honest house-owning citizens. If they had relied upon the state to supply all the building materials they needed, their houses would probably never have been finished, for the simple reason that most supplies are requisitioned the moment they become available by municipal housing organizations. Thus, they turned to the black market for almost anything from carpenter's screws to tiles. The effect of the new law was to reduce severely the construction of private housing in 1964 without producing a corresponding increase in municipal housing. Kosygin brought all this to an end. "The state is to help future house owners with long-term loans, supplies of building materials and provision of utility services," he said. This was followed up by "unofficial" attacks in the press on "snoopers" who sought to bring house owners to trial for their property.

13

RETURN TO
THE SHADOWS

BY THE END of June, 1965, Moscow was again full of rumors of political unrest. A meeting of the Communist party's Central Committee had been called for October, which was to attempt finally to settle the dispute between the economic progressives and the conservatives. Then, it was postponed for unexplained reasons, and stories began to circulate of a new power struggle taking place in the Kremlin. The progressives, as we have already seen, were trying to throw away the more stifling dogmas of Russian Communism of the past, and to substitute in their place an increasingly flexible and pragmatic attitude toward the nation's urgent economic and social problems, among the party, the Government and the civil service; and as they began to consolidate their position, the conservatives fought back, regarding any threat to the centralized administration as a threat to the whole Soviet system, and seeing any major change in the ordinances laid down by Lenin, Stalin, and to a lesser extent, Khrushchev, as an ideological capitulation to the West.

Some progressives who had originally supported reform had been frightened, it seemed, by the extent to which it had been taken in such a short period of time, and were beginning to side with the conservatives. Some "usually well-informed sources"—those unidentifiable shadows in communion with journalists and diplomats in Moscow—claimed that Brezhnev was among them, and might soon be rejoining his old master, in premature retirement. They suggested he was to be replaced by Alexander Shelepin, the ex-head of the secret police. But other, apparently equally well-informed, sources said that Shelepin had been arrested, and thus removed from the political arena. Whatever the truth might eventually prove to be, it was undoubtedly Shelepin's figure that was now looming over the whole scene.

Even before the coup, he had wielded vast authority. He had reorganized the secret police for Khrushchev, and then left his protégé, Vladimir Semichastny (who had been his deputy in the Young Communist League earlier), in charge of it under his general supervision. He had become chairman of the Committee for Party-State Control, a large, independent organization working semisecretly within the organs of the party and the Government, investigating official conduct and reporting its findings exclusively to Shelepin himself, who was in turn answerable only to the Presidium. Most important of all, he had also been appointed party secretary responsible for the political supervision of all the armed forces and the police, both plain-clothed and uniformed. As a result of all these duties, he had been co-opted on the Council of Ministers as a deputy-premier.

Now, he was a member of the Presidium. He had been elevated to a place in this supreme organ exactly a month after Khrushchev had been expelled from it;

leading several Western commentators to suggest, rather feebly, that this was his reward for co-operating in the coup. In fact, for a man of his power, it was a promotion overdue, and made all the more logical by the unique position he now proved to be in, to uproot the influence of Khrushchev from the midst of Soviet officialdom, as, on Khrushchev's behalf seven years before, he had partially uprooted that of Stalin and Beria from the secret police. On account of his career as Stalin's last organizer of the Young Communist League and Khrushchev's head of secret police, Western commentators have also regarded him as an extremely sinister, not to say unpleasant, figure in Russian politics, and have attributed to him the opinions held by the reactionaries who were opposing reform. If Kosygin's promotion could be considered a step forward toward the full realization of civilization in Russia, they argued, Shelepin's threatened to be a far greater one, backward to Stalinism. But it must be said that if Shelepin had worked under Stalin without open complaint, then so had all the other surviving members of the Soviet hierarchy; and that if he had run the secret police, then several other equally prominent colleagues of his had been closely associated with its activities and had given them, at the least, their tacit approval. If he had been outwardly loyal to Khrushchev until he was near his end, then Brezhnev and Kosygin had been as well.

Shelepin's career has combined the elements of both a modern liberal and an old-guard reactionary. Unlike most of his colleagues, he was born—in 1918—into a middle-class family, the son of a senior railway official. He studied at one of the most prestigious schools of higher education in the country: the Moscow Institute of History, Philosophy and Literature, which provided him with an intellectual background vastly different from those which Brezhnev and Kosygin had acquired at the Kursk Institute of Land Utilization and Reclamation and the Leningrad Textile Institute respectively. Shelepin and his contemporaries there were acutely conscious of their elite status, and it was from these institutes that the first concerted criticism of the Soviet practice of Marxism-Leninism began to emerge in the mid-fifties. Many of his fellow students became academicians and a few of them writers, and it was undeniable that Shelepin was probably as a result the only leading politician in the Soviet Union with a genuine understanding of the intellectual mood.

He became a professional politician immediately he graduated in 1939, and was sent as a political instructor to the troops on the Finnish front. Returning to Moscow a year later, he became a member of the Communist party at the remarkably young age of twenty-two. (Most Russians maintain their membership in the Young Communist League until they reach the age of compulsory resignation at twenty-eight, and take no further part in political activity.)

Shelepin worked as an official in the Moscow branch of the Young Communist League, enjoying in these last years of Stalin's reign successive promotions until, shortly before the dictator's death, he was appointed in 1952 as head of the whole national movement, becoming a full member of the Communist party's Central Committee at the same time. When Stalin died, and while others were still in power, Shelepin was marked as one of Khrushchev's most important devotees. Although Molotov strongly opposed the Virgin Lands scheme, Shelepin arranged for the mobilization of 350,000 Young Communist League volunteers (a term which should be interpreted in its military sense) to go to the east and work for its fulfillment. In 1956, he arranged for another 300,000 to leave urban Russia and serve the state on construction projects in Siberia and in the north; and a year later, he drafted 600,000 secondary-school dropouts, on Khrushchev's request, into livestock husbandry, many of whom would otherwise have taken jobs in industry.

Before he left the Young Communist movement in 1958, Shelepin complained to its Twelfth Congress that too many of its members had been ill educated in Communist principles. "Some young men and women, and above all some students," he said, "have made negative remarks that have belittled the achievements of the Soviet people, and distorted the truths about Soviet life. Some youth organizations at times forget about the influence of the frenzied propaganda which is being conducted against the Soviet Union by imperialists in capitalist states. People can still be found who bite this bourgeois bait, and find themselves captivated by alien attractions, such as vulgar dances, abstract paintings and sculptures and ostentatious clothes." Many of those he complained against he had already had sent to work away from such temptations on Khrushchev's projects in the east. Now, he went briefly to the Central Committee headquarters to exhort their elders to follow.

By the end of the year, Shelepin was head of the secret police; and in that capacity, he presented the Twenty-second Congress of the Communist party a report on the atrocities committed by his predecessors. Perhaps his most shocking addition to the revelations

Khrushchev had already made was his account of how Kaganovich used to scrawl "Fuck you" across the pleas for clemency which he received from political prisoners sentenced to death. But although he worked hard to remove the worst abuses of secret police powers in Russia, he also showed himself to be a stern disciplinarian. He had been one of those directly responsible, he implied, for two of the most savage laws passed under Khrushchev: the first giving local authorities the power to exile citizens who refused to engage themselves in "socially useful labor" to the east, and the second making embezzlement by economic officials a capital offense.

Since Khrushchev's fall, however, Shelepin has gone out of his way to align himself with the liberals, as, equally surprisingly, his predecessor Beria had done after Stalin's death, and his Committee for Party-State Control has become one of the most active pressure groups for economic reform. Its reports have criticized several Government agencies for their neglect of light industries, particularly those producing textiles and durable consumer goods. The committee has admonished the authorities to "pay due attention to these important matters" and particularly to the low level of technical and scientific knowledge within the industries "which lag far behind that of other branches of the economy." The whole structure of technical colleges and research institutes should be re-examined, with the needs of light industry very much in mind, and additional funds and equipment should be allocated for their expansion.

Another campaign initiated by Shelepin has emphasized the importance of another field greatly neglected in the past: the service trades. Drawing attention to the poor standards of efficiency and courtesy in these occupations, and the low morale among people employed in them, the committee has said—in contradiction of much that has been said by internal Soviet propaganda in the past—that "workers in canteens and laundries, in hair-dressing establishments and retail shops do not produce material wealth. But they are engaged in no less responsible tasks than those who make steel and mine coal, grow grain and build ships. In our country, everybody works for the welfare of the people."

These statements may lead one to the conclusion that Shelepin has undergone a change of heart too rapidly to be convincing. But such reversals are by no means unknown to Soviet politics, and they have often been signs in the past that the person involved in them was actively maneuvering for power. Perhaps Shelepin has already advanced his cause too far, too quickly, and he has already been removed; perhaps he is to replace Brezhnev; perhaps there never was any conflict between them in the first place. For Westerners, the central truth about Soviet politics remains the same under the new regime as it was under the old: almost nothing is certain, and almost anything can happen without the West having the slightest hint of it.

By the end of June, Nikita Khrushchev himself had moved with his wife Nina into a five-room apartment, next door to the Canadian Embassy in Moscow, overlooking a quiet, tree-lined street about a mile from the Kremlin. Western correspondents knew the address, but none of them had succeeded in achieving access even to the hallway on the ground floor; even Richard Nixon was turned away by the woman caretaker, who protested that Khrushchev had gone out and was not expected back for a long time. But he has been seen twice since his fall: once, in March, when he had gone to vote in the elections in his old constituency of the Kalinin district of Moscow, when he said that he was "living the sort of life that pensioners live" and that his health was "not bad"; and once, about a month later, at an exhibition in the Manège hall, when he told Ian Brodie of the *London Daily Express* and Lars Bringert of the *Stockholm Dagens Nyheter* that he still believed in peaceful coexistence. The rest has been silence.

INDEX

Abrasimov, Pyotr A., 148
Adenauer, Konrad, 128
ADN (East German news agency), 148
Adzhubei, Alexei, 28-31, 35, 44, 57, 63, 106, 190, 193
Africa, 78, 89
Agitprop, 173
Agriculture, 26-28, 35, 40, 56, 57-58, 99-106, 176-78, 191; Brezhnev on, 180, 205-7; collectivization of, 99-103, 153, 165-67, 205-7; K.'s knowledge of, 156; since K., 205-7; Virgin Lands project (*see* Virgin Lands)
Agricultural Inst. (Moscow), 173
Albania, 150, 151
All-Union Party Congress, 159
American Broadcasting Company, 18
"Antiparty group," 35, 178
Anti-Semitism, 78, 82, 91, 129
Armenia Radio, 103-4, 105, 138
Army, Red, 48, 49, 52, 53, 59, 210
Art, artists, 29, 47, 89-94, 132; Polish, 142
Asia, 26, 78
Associated Press, 128
Australia, 104
Australian National University, 114
Automobiles, 45, 97, 98, 162

Babii Yar, 91

Baikonur spacedrome, 33
Belgrade, 97-98
Belyayev, Nikolai, 177-78
Beria, Lavrenti P., 46, 176, 214
Berlin, 139, 148
Black marketeers, 73, 75
Black Sea, 21 ff, 47, 99
Bolsheviks, 158, 163, 164, 172, 173; Kosygin and, 182. *See also* Revolution, Bolshevik
Bonn, 128
Bratsk hydroelectric scheme, 72, 94
Bread shortages, 100-1, 176, 193
Brezhnev (son of Leonid I.), 180
Brezhnev, Galina, 180
Brezhnev, Leonid I., 131, 132, 167, 169-81, 188; background, biography, 169-81; and China, 141, 143, 152; and East Europe, 138-39, 141, 144, 146, 147, 148; as First Secretary, 19-20, 169 ff; and K., 24, 27-28, 39, 48, 52-53, 171-72, 175, 179; and new mood in Russia, 190 ff, 210, 211, 215
Brezhnev, Mrs. Leonid (Victoria), 180
Brezhnev, Mikhail, 181
Brijoni, Isle of, 98
Bringert, Lars, 216
Brodie, Ian, 216
Bucharest, 110
Budapest, 144-47
Budapest Radio, 146-47

Bulganin, Nikolai A., 35
Bulgaria, 89, 139, 149-51

Canada, 104
Cape Kennedy, 33
Cape Pitsunda, 22-34, 37, 44
Castro, Fidel, 45, 88
Censorship, press, 77 ff, 127; self-imposed, 77, 78, 115
Central Committee, CPSU, 53, 90, 122, 123-24, 130, 150, 161, 165, 190-91; Brezhnev appointed to, 176; and economic reforms, 199-201, 209; K. and, 18-20, 36, 41, 43-49, 50, 53-65, 178; Kosygin appointed to, 183; Presidium of (*see* Presidium); Shelepin appointed to, 212, 213
Central Statistics Board, 203
Central Telegraph, 77
China, 39, 40, 88, 103, 127; K. and, 40, 41, 61, 62, 63, 86, 96, 116-17, 140, 141, 144; reaction to K.'s dismissal in, 151-52
Chou En-lai, 116
Christians, 82
CIA, 109, 113-14
Clothing, 86, 107, 183, 202-4
Coexistence, 92-93, 129, 132, 145
Cold War, 76, 127, 143-44
Collective farming, 99-103, 153, 165-67, 205-7. *See also* Agriculture
"Collective leadership," 42, 56-57, 118, 131, 176; Brezhnev and Kosygin's, 171
Comecon, 96-97
Committee and memorandum, rule by, 170-71
Commitee for Party-State Control, 43, 210
Common Market, 97
Communist (periodical), 199
Congresses, CPSU: Second, 181-82; Twelfth, 213; Nineteenth, 176; Twentieth, 177, 187-88; Twenty-second, 188, 213

Consumer goods, 31, 32, 69, 85-86, 204. *See also* Shortages
Co-operatives, Kosygin and, 182-83
Correspondents, Soviet. *See* Newspapers, Soviet
Correspondents, Western, 11-20, 70-89, 108-24 (*see also* Newspapers, Western; specific individuals); K. and, 98-99, 120-21, 216; political jokes and, 103-6
Cosmonauts, 19, 33-38
Council of Ministers, CPSU, 121-22, 184, 187, 210; and K.'s dismissal, 19-20, 31, 47, 56-57, 64-65
CPSU (Communist Party of the Soviet Union), 108-24, 190-216 *passim*
Crimea, 99
Crop failures, 57, 99-103, 165. *See also* Agriculture
Cuba, 12, 62, 78, 121; aid to, 88
Cult of personality (cult of the individual), 40, 56-57, 131, 145, 171; Kosygin speech on, 188
Cyrankiewicz, Josef, 144
Czechoslovakia, 149

Daily Worker (British), 130-31
Defense, Ministry of, 176
Defense industry, W. W. II, 184-85
Denmark, 128
Deportation, 72-73, 178, 214
De-Stalinization process. *See under* Stalin
Diplomatic experts, 110-15, 117, 127-28
Dneprodzerzhinsk, 172, 174, 175
Dobrynin, Anatoly F., 129
Don Basin, 156
Dorticos, Osvaldo, 12
DPA (West German news agency), 17-18
Dudintsev, Vladimir, 90, 195-96

East Europe, 58, 68, 79, 89, 105 (*see also* specific countries, individuals); reaction to K.'s dismissal in, 139-51

East Germany, 63, 139, 147-48

Economic Council, CPSU, 184

Economic policies, 132; K.'s, 31-32, 35, 44, 55-59, 64, 105-6; since K., 197-208, 209-16

Education: compulsory, Kosygin and, 185; dropouts, 213; K.'s, 155-56, 159, 160-61; religious, forbidden, 82; scientific, Shelepin on, 214

Eisenhower, Dwight D., 59

Embassies in Moscow, 110, 115

Embezzlement, 43, 214

Émigré groups, 72, 74, 81, 174, 189

Erhard, Ludwig, 63

Evening Moscow, 162

Expulsion of Western correspondents, 16, 77, 78, 99

Fedorenko, Nikolai T., 203

Feoktistov, Constantin, 33

Finance, ministry of, 187

Five-year plans, 32, 58, 87, 184

Food: distribution, Kosygin and, 187; shortages, 42, 85, 86, 99-103, 132-33, 206

Foreign aid programs, Soviet, 87-89, 97, 128

Foreign Ministry, Soviet, 57, 117; and journalists' difficulties, 70, 71, 77, 103, 119, 121

Foreign Trade, Ministry of, 74

France, 15, 89, 129, 130

Furtseva, Yekaterina, 91

Gagarin, Yuri, 34, 87

Gagra, K. at, 22

Gaulle, Charles de, 38, 125, 181

Genetics. *See* Lysenko, Trofim D.

Georgia, Stalin and, 154

Germany, 63, 87, 142, 174-75, 185. *See also* East Germany;

Nazis; West Germany; World War II

Gold reserves, 105

Gollan, John, 130-31

Gomulka, Wladislaw, 17, 45, 139-45

Gori (Georgia), 154

Gorki, experimental farm at, 196

Goryunov, Dmitri, 17

Grain production, 26, 99-103, 104-5, 177, 193. *See also* Agriculture

Great Britain, 11, 58, 89, 119-20, 198; Communist party in, 21, 130-31; Kremlinology in, 108, 112, 113, 119; reaction to K.'s dismissal in, 21, 68-69, 127, 128-29, 130-31

Gromyko, Andrei, 30, 120, 121

Guerrilla warfare, 165, 175

GUM, 135

Harvest failures, 57, 99-103, 165. *See also* Agriculture

Harriman, Averell, 179

History of the Communist Party of the Soviet Union, 126

Hitler, Adolf, 175. *See also* Nazis

Housing, 29-30, 59, 84, 107; since K., 207-8

Hughes, John, 156-57

Hungary, 36, 79, 139, 140, 144-47

Ilyichev, Leonid, 54

India, 63, 128

Industry, 31-32, 40, 56, 58-59, 105, 132; Kosygin and, 184-86, 187; since K., 197-205, 214-15

Institute of Engineering (Kharkov), 199

Institute of Genetics, 194-95, 196

Institute of Land Utilization and Reclamation, 156, 172-73

Intellectuals, 132, 138, 212. *See also* Art, artists

International Women's Day, 133

Intourist, 73, 81, 115
Irkutsk, 182
Italy, 32, 55, 130, 162
Izvestia, 52, 74, 75, 181; Adzhubei and, 28-29, 43-44, 52, 74, 75, 190; on day K. fell, 14-15, 53

Jaffe, Sam, 18
Japan, 58, 60-61
Jehovah's Witnesses, 82
Jenkins, Walter, 12
Jews, 78, 82, 91, 129, 174
John XXIII, Pope, 63
Johnson, Lyndon B., 11-12, 129, 149
Jokes, political, 54, 69-70, 95-96, 103-6, 138

Kadar, Janos, 36, 45, 139-46
Kaganovich, Lazar, 158, 160, 161, 214
Kalinin district (Moscow), 216
Kalinovka (Ukraine), 153-54, 182
Kazakhstan, 45, 72, 102, 137; K. sends Brezhnev to, 176-77
Kennedy, John F., 62, 192
Kennedy, Robert, 143
Kharkov, 197, 199
Kharlamov, Mikhail, 44, 191
Khrushchev, Ksenia, 104, 158
Khrushchev, Leonid, 158
Khrushchev, Nikita S.: birth, background, early days, education, 153-68; jokes about (*see* Jokes, political); policies of (*see* Agriculture; Economic policies; Industry; etc.); public opinion of (*see* Public opinion); and specific agencies, events, individuals, etc. (*see by name*)
Khrushchev, Nina Petrovna, 24, 62, 65, 169, 215
Khrushchev, Rada, 29, 62
Khrushchev, Sergei (father of Nikita), 153, 155, 156

Khrushchev, Sergei (son of Nikita), 61
Kiev, 23, 81, 129, 160, 163, 197
Kirilenko, Andrei, 39
Klin, 72
Komarov, Vladimir, 33
Komsomolskaya Pravda, 51, 53, 195
Konev, I. S., 52
Koslov, Frol, 179; at K.'s dismissal, 37, 42-43
Kossior, Stanislav, 163, 164
Kosygin, Alexei N., 19-20, 132, 167, 169-71, 181-89; background, biography, 181-89; and China, 141, 143, 151; and East Europe, 138-39, 146, 147; and K., 27-28, 31-32, 39, 52-53, 181, 188; and new mood in Russia, 190-204, 211; as Prime Minister, 169-71, 188-89
Kotor (Yugoslavia), 98
Krag, Jens Otto, 129
Kremlin, 67, 70, 120, 169; Western attempts at understanding, 108-24
Kremlinology, 108-24, 138
Kuban, 99
Kungurtsev, Sergei, 189
Kursk, 156, 173
Kutuzovsky Prospect, 46
Kuznetsov, Alexander, 186

Labor camps, 46, 72-73, 83, 164, 165
Lebedev, Vladimir, 191
Lenin, Vladimir I., 42, 123, 157, 181-82; and Stalin, 159, 163
Leningrad, 81, 137, 183, 184; Stalin's purge in, 186
Liberman, Yevsei, 197-204
Life magazine, 120
Literaturnaya Gazeta, 196
Livestock, 57, 101-2, 206, 213
Lobanov, Pavel, 196-97

London, 11, 15, 113, 119-20; reaction to K.'s fall, 68-69, 127, 128
London Daily Express, 216
London Evening News, 11-13, 15
Louis, Victor, 11-13, 15-16
Lvov, 204
Lysenko, Trofim D., 192-97

Malenkov, Georgi M., 176, 178, 186
Malinovsky, Rodion, 48, 112-13
Malyshev, Ivan, 203-4
Management: agricultural, 26-27, 56, 57-58 (*see also* Agriculture); industrial, 56, 57 ff. (*see also* Industry)
Managerial class, Soviet, 69, 197
Manège, the, 47, 90, 216
Mao Tse-tung, 40, 62, 88, 116; on K.'s 70th birthday, 69
Marxism-Leninism, 40, 85, 123, 129, 137, 157; Shelepin and, 212
Matthews, Mervyn, 73
May Day, 109, 152
Mayak (Lighthouse) men's tailoring plant, 202-3
Meetings between Russians and Westerners, 70-75
Metallurgical Institute, 173
Metro (Moscow), 161
Middle East, 89
Middleton, Drew, 127
Mikoyan, Anastas, 12, 39, 180, 184, 185, 186; attempts to mediate with K., 25, 30-31, 34-36
Minsk, 81
Misconceptions about Russia, 82-83
Mogilev, 101
Moldavia, 175
Molotov, V. M., 35, 104, 176, 178; Kosygin attack on, 188
Molotov-Ribbentrop pact, 164
Monde, Le, 54
Monks, monasteries, 165

Moscow, 12 ff, 81 ff, 133, 161-62, 166; housing in, 29-30; at K.'s dismissal, 12-20, 22-23, 135-37; Kremlinology in, 108-24, 138. *See also* Kremlin
Moscow City Soviet, 29-30, 162
Moscow Institute of History, Philosophy and Literature, 211-12
Moscow Radio, 12, 34, 78, 125, 141
Moslems, 82
Munich, 109, 139
Munitions industry, Kosygin's W. W. II activity in, 184-85

National Economic Council, 204
National Security Agency, U.S., 109
NATO, 52, 127-28
Navy, Soviet, 63
Nazis, 50, 91, 150, 164-65, 194
Nemchinov, Vasily, 199, 200
New Arbat (Moscow), 46
New York, 15, 20, 115
New York Stock Exchange, 20
New York Times, 127, 137
Newspapers, East European, 68
Newspapers, Soviet, 28-29, 36, 53, 70, 74-75, 79, 191-92; political reporting in, 118; public discontent with, 85. *See also* specific news agencies, newspapers
Newspapers, Western, 11-20, 54, 68-69, 70-89; Kremlinology and, 108-24
Newsweek, 103
Nixon, Richard, 215
Norwegian State Broadcasting Corp., 44, 191
Not by Bread Alone, 90, 195
Novocherkassk, 42
Novorossisk, 174
Novosti Press Agency, 110
Novotný, Antonín, 149
Nuns, 165
Nyezvestny (sculptor), 91-92

Olshansky, Mikhail, 195
One Day in the Life of Ivan Denisovich, 90
Oslo (Norway), 191

Palewsky, M. Gaston, 36-38
Paris, 15, 129, 192
Party Life, 127
Peasants, 27-28, 101, 166-67; K. and, 153, 155, 166-67, 206-7
Petrograd, 182
Petrovsko-Maryinsk district, 159
Planning, economic, Liberman and, 197-204
Podgorny, Nikolai, 25, 39
Poets, 91-94
Poland, 17, 89, 139-46
Polish Daily, 142
Politburos: East Germany, 148; Polish, 145; Russian (*see* Presidium)
Polyansky, Dmitri S., 64
Pompidou, Georges, 129
Ponomarenko, Danteleimon, 176-77
Postyshev, Konstantin, 163
Potansky, Dmitri, 39
Pravda, 15, 19, 44, 51-52, 53, 192; accuses K., 126, 147; Liberman in, 199-200
Presidium, CPSU (formerly Politburo), 53, 123-24, 163, 164; and collective leadership, 171 (*see also* Collective leadership); K. and, 20, 21, 25, 31, 35-65 *passim*, 113-15, 116, 123-24, 163, 164, 176; Shelepin and, 210-11; since K., 210-11
Private ownership, 206-7
Profit system, 132, 198 ff
Proletariat, 137
Propaganda and Agitation Dept., Central Committee, 190-91
Prostitutes, 72-73
Public opinion, 132-34; K. and, 80, 84-94, 96-106, 107-8, 116. *See also* Jokes, political

Public relations campaigns, 105-6, 132-34
Purges, 105, 160-68 *passim*, 186. *See also* Deportation
Pushkin, Alexander S., 153

Racialism, 78. *See also* Anti-Semitism
Radio, Communist, 12, 34, 44, 78, 103-4, 105, 109, 191. *See also* Armenia Radio; Budapest Radio; Moscow Radio; etc.
Radio Free Europe, 109, 139, 142
Rationing, 100. *See also* Shortages
Red Star, 109
Reuters news bureau (Moscow), 196
Religion, 40, 78, 82, 165. *See also* Anti-Semitism
Restaurants, 133
Reston, James, 137
Revisionists, 90, 151
Revolution, Bolshevik, 133, 158, 159, 163, 182
Revolution Day, 133
Rigby, Thomas, 114-15
Ruhr, 58
Rumania, 62, 109-10, 139, 141
Russian Secretariat, Great Britain's, 110
Russian Federation, 39, 185
Russian Orthodox Church, 40

St. Petersburg, 182
Salinger, Pierre, 192
San Francisco Stock Exchange, 20
Satyukov, Victor, 44, 52, 192
Scandinavian tour, K.'s, 61
Science, new Russian mood in, 192 ff, 214
Secrecy, governmental, 119. *See also* Kremlinology
Secret police, 15, 43, 44, 53, 83; and correspondents, 71-72; K.'s reform of, 46; Shelepin and, 46, 210, 211, 213-14

Semichastny, Vladimir, 43, 44, 46-47, 210
Service trades, 214-15
Seventh-Day Adventists, 82
Shapiro, Henry, 18
Shelepin, Alexander, 43, 46, 210-16
Shoe industry, 186, 204
Shortages, 42, 85-86, 99-103, 104; Kosygin and, 183, 186
Shuysky, Alexander, 191
Shvernik, Nikolai, 39
Siberia, 45, 102, 182-83, 213; labor camps in, 46, 72, 83, 164
Siberian Territorial Union of Co-operatives, 183
Smith, Joseph, 139
Social-Democrat Labor Party, 181, 182
Sofia, 139, 151
Soldatov, Alexander, 128
Solzhenitsyn, Alexander, 90
Soviet Committee of Women, 62
Soviet History of the Great Patriotic War, 185
Soviet Union, 190
Soviet-United States Friendship Society, 62
Sovietology. See Kremlinology
Space programs, 33-38, 87-88
Speech, freedom of, 82
Sputnik I, 87
Stalin, Josef V., 40, 42, 46, 51, 68, 72, 96, 104, 154, 159, 167, 169-70, 182; Brezhnev and, 176; and cult of personality, 40 (see also Cult of personality); death of, 14, 129, 135, 167; de-Stalinization, 51, 72, 90, 94, 96, 104, 130, 154; K. and, 23, 84, 104, 160-70 passim; Kosygin and, 181, 183, 185-88; Lysenko and, 193, 194, 197
Stalingrad, 81; Battle of, 165
Stalinists, 138, 159, 167-68
Stalino, 160

Standard of living, 99, 106, 187, 207-8
Staraya Square, 18, 54
State Committee for Defense (W. W. II), 164
State Committee for Radio and Television, 44, 191
State Planning Committee (Gosplan), 31-32, 188, 197
State receptions, Moscow, 120, 169, 178
Stepakov, Vladimir, 190
Stock exchanges, 20, 128
Stockholm Dagens Nyheter, 216
Strikes, 30, 101, 157-58
Students: Polish, 142; Soviet, 137-38, 154; visiting, 78, 80-81
Suslov, Mikhail, 90, 131; and K.'s dismissal, 39-42, 54-63, 191
Supreme Soviet, 64, 123, 178, 185, 204
Svanidze, Catherine (wife of Stalin), 182

TASS, 34, 60, 78, 110, 119; and K.'s dismissal, 17, 19-20
Tatu, Michel, 54
Tbilisi (Georgia), 154
Television, K. appears on, 106
Textile industry: after K., 202-3; Kosygin and, 183-84, 189
Times of London, 68-69
Tirana (Albania) Radio, 151
Tito, Josip Broz, 96-98, 141
Tourists, 80-83, 133
Trapeznikov, Valery, 199, 200
Trevelyn, Sir Humphrey, 113
Tryankovsky, Oleg, 191
Turkey, 150

Ukraine, 153-60, 163-66, 167-68, 204; anti-Semitism in, 78, 91, 129; grain production in, 99; in W. W. II, 48, 50-52, 174-75
Ukrainian Party Congress, 159
Ulbricht, Walter, 148, 180
Union of Writers, 93-94, 142, 166

United Nations, 60
United Press International, 18, 128, 139
United States, 11-12, 58, 60, 128-29, 149, 198; and Kremlinology, 108-10, 113-15; and nuclear war, 52; space program, 33; U-2 incident, 120; and Yugoslavia, 97
United States Information Service, 114
USSR magazine, 191-92
U-2 spy plane incident, 120

Vavilov, Nikolai, 194, 195, 196
Victory in Europe Day, 133
Vietnam, 121
Vinogradev, Sergei S., 129
Virgin Lands project, 26-28, 35, 102-3, 176-78, 212-13
Voronov, Gennadi, 39
Voroshilov, K. Y., 178
Voskhod I, 33-38
Voznesensky, Nikolai, 186

Warsaw, 139-40, 141-44
Warsaw Radio, 141
Washington, D.C., 12, 113-14, 128, 129. *See also* United States
West, the: Communists in, 21, 129-32 (*see also* specific countries); correspondents, newspapers (*see* Correspondents, Western; Newspapers, West-

ern); difficulties in understanding Russia in, 70-89, 108-24; reaction to K.'s dismissal in, 125-34, 135-37, 149 (*see also* specific countries)
West German news agencies, 17, 137
West Germany, 58, 63, 128
Wilson, Harold, 129
"Workers' Universities," 159
World War I, 158
World War II, 48, 50-52, 63, 81, 87; Brezhnev in, 174-75; death of K.'s son in, 158; K.'s activity during, 164-65; Kosygin in, 184-86
Writers, 61, 89-94, 142, 166

Yegorov, Boris, 33
Yepishev, A. A., 51, 53
Yevtushenko, Yevgeny, 90-94
Young Communist League, 43, 51, 102, 106, 123, 193; on K.'s fall, 149; Shelepin and, 210, 211, 212-13
Yugoslavia, 79; K. visits, 96-99
Yuzovka, 104, 156-57, 160

Zamyatin, Leonid, 17-18
Zavidovo, 23
Zhdanov, Andrei, 183, 186
Zhivkov, Todor, 150-51
Zhukov, Constantin, 48